ULTRARUNNING
MY STORY

By Mike Bouscaren

Front cover photo credit to Will LaFollette

Background photo credit to Greg A. Hartford
From AcadiaMagic.com

ISBN: 1-4196-7113-8

Printed in the United States of America

ULTRARUNNING: WHERE, HOW, WHY

There's always someone who knows more, or has run more, or can run faster. That's not me, but I do have twenty-five personal stories to share. They describe ultrarunning events from 50 kilometers to 100 miles, and a few marathons, too. You'll see different venues, how to train, equipment that works effectively, and how to plan logistics. Why do people run ultras? The practice of long distance running develops proficiencies of body and mind that facilitate everything we do.

Ultrarunning holds a secret. People who know the secret are possessive of its charm: it's not by running long that we see different things; it's by running long that we see things differently. Long distance travel by foot is another form of vacationing, whose Latin root "vacare" means "to be empty." In this way we travel, arriving in a different place, not a physical place. That is the secret.

By sharing this, I feared that my companion ultrarunners would be mad at me, that our secret would be lost. Then I remembered how hard it is to run an ultramarathon, especially our sport's signature one hundred mile distance. People can read about this special kind of travel, but will find it difficult to experience for themselves. In that way I am confident we will keep our secret, even after it's been told.

My run stories appear chronologically, except in Chapter One, where I have taken three of them forward in a recollection to introduce the concept of ultrarunning's Magic. I learned about Magic in my third year of ultrarunning, and it became the key driver in my journey of self-discovery.

Words are merely thought images. My thought images became clearer to me as the journey progressed; so too, my writing turned more precise in describing the connections of body and mind, as understood by experiencing the Magic.

"Ultrarunning: My Story" is presented exactly as it happened. The work of gaining High Ground was difficult and repetitive; my recollections of each run experience turn more evocative as I more completely seize on their meaning. As I had to be, the reader should also be patient. The runner, the writer, and the person all went together on this Magical journey, and the reader is invited to see how they all change, as the secret of ultrarunning becomes clear.

TABLE OF CONTENTS

CHAPTER ONE – FLASHBACK

When I began to extend beyond the 26.2 mile marathon distance, I was a still pusher. We learn to push before we understand. First in line, first in class, first to finish: I – push myself, driven to win. Pushers have resistance in front of them – me. They are acquisitive – mine. They can never get enough and are never satisfied. Directed by the past, pushers are destined to repeat it.

I evolved into a puller. Instinctively, we know this is good; that's why people say, "We're pulling for you." Pullers put resistance behind them; leaning forward in the running stride, pullers allow gravity to help. Pullers find economies of thought and motion; they become lighter in self with directed energy. Inquisitive and with the past in their wake, pullers are satisfied with the air they breathe.

BEETHOVEN APPEARS AT MOUNT TOBY
August 27, 2006

I surge higher, arms, legs, and heart pumping near the anaerobic threshold. Lead runners begin tumbling down from the summit, and I'm passing people going up. The physicality here is dense – all 134 competitors pressed together on this steep hill, this final assault to and from the top.

In the transition to a steeper incline, my breathing moves from unnoticed accompaniment to the prominent feature: deep, rapid, full. This envelops me – I am hard breathing, only that, body and mind reduced to pointed focus.

I hear someone close behind, drafting. I do not look, but use him to force me deeper into the tunnel of concentration. We are two made greater than one; this is turning sublime. I slow, near exhaustion as the hill gets even steeper, still pumping at the edge, still forced, still passing. This is the wild boundary between overload and extinction. He passes me. I thank him, saying, "Good job." He says the same to me. We continue surging, now me in pursuit – it doesn't matter who's first.

It's the 19th annual Mount Toby Trail Run, in the beautiful Berkshires, fourteen miles of fast-poured fun. I haven't run this one before or entered an event this short in almost twenty years. More typically I go a longer distance, at a slower pace. From the start it's up tempo; from the start I wonder if I can hold this tempo through to the finish.

Coming down the steep, I throttle back for control while others fly past, feet touch-braking on the rocks in fraction-second intervals. What is this but mad, gone-native atavism? My mind is wide open – to the possibility of finishing strong or crashing, to the possibility of anything. What's already happened feels beyond possibility, and there's more. Seven runners have passed me coming down from the top, and I have passed five of them back. The last one I pass says something unintelligible to me, as if in a foreign tongue. I trip and fall forward in a well-practiced shoulder roll, my CamelBak cushioning against the rock surface. I'm up in a second, pressing on, hard-breathing, only that; the foreign tongue fades farther back. I run possessed. "This is more than just me running," I think.

My previous results have taught me to estimate a finishing time by multiplying the place of recent years' last finishers by point eight; that factored place is where I typically end up. From the 2005 event times, my interpolated goal is two hours, thirty-seven minutes.

I don't look at my watch. I'm close to the finish and run as hard as I can all the way through. In the final two minutes, rain sheets down – nature's curtain close on this wild, impromptu theater, now after two hours, twenty-seven. With posting of the final results, I'm spot on my point eight estimated place among all finishers. But why is this ten minutes faster than last year's eightieth percentile time?

Coincidence or karma? In the same time frame, thirty miles distant at Tanglewood, the Boston Symphony Orchestra launches into Beethoven's Seventh Symphony. Driving home through blue-green hills, I hear it, time delayed, on the radio. The first movement is a heroically staged introduction that reminds me of putting on my running gear in the car before the Mount Toby start. The second movement carries an epic mood of anticipation, much like standing in the crowd of amped-up runners near the starting line before we're sent off. The third, called "presto" or fast, is the adrenalin-loaded first few miles, not completely purposeful, but completely energetic, extending to a more measured pace in recall of the effort's immensity. The music, the run: it's happening again – they're the same thing.

The final movement, called "allegretto con brio" or quickly with vigor, is the hyperventilating ascent to the top, the anaerobic finish. Beethoven surges into note compression, the orchestra's interplay leaves no space without sound – I think he's possibly crazy and probably deaf, so enthralled with the notes he cannot hear, that he releases all inhibition and form, stroking down as many as he can in a short space – my steps descending – so wild – now I'm speeding back down Mount Toby, speeding in the car, passing on the left and the right, carried in Beethoven's deaf, mad, certain mind – I look down at the speedo, and it reads one-oh-five – holy shit !

He composed it nearly two hundred years ago. Today, he cast his energy over us as we ran in a pack; free thinking, like-minded souls, up Mount Toby and down again. The Tanglewood performance is spiritual Doppler effect: in one place a spell is cast, while some distance away, its magical impact reverberates.

I'd finished dozens of marathons and ultramarathons before the Mount Toby event. Most people understand time and space literally or in the context of imagined physical limitations. Running ultras changes that, as the consequence of routinely extending beyond those limits.

———

FINDING MAGIC ON CATALINA ISLAND

The runner holds his transistor radio like a bowl of soup, arm extended. I hear show tunes. Slowly passing him, I wait for a moment of recognition; then, "Are you going to listen to the Yankees game later?"

"Yep."

That was in the early miles of my first 50k (31 miles) in 1999, the Sybil Ludington 50k, on country roads near New York City.

New to ultras, I went back to Stan Jensen's Run100's website in search of more exotic venues, thinking, "Maybe if the scenery's nicer, it'll take my mind's foot off the pain pedal a little."

That's where I saw photos of the free range buffalo on Catalina Island, California:

Most people would agree that running with buffalos would be more exciting than running with transistor radios. So I ramped up my distances, running four more ultras in the next eighteen months, and went to Catalina Island in 2001 for what turned out to be its last 100k (62.1 mile) event, and my first.

Race director Baz Hawley introduces the notion of "Magic" at the Friday night pasta feed, to describe what can happen when you run on Catalina. And I meet running greats Scott Jurek and Henri Girault, different types of record setters: Scott, the future winner of seven consecutive Western States 100's; and Henri, to complete over 500 100k events. I'm in heavy company for a newbie, yet everyone's friendly as a neighbor.

East Coast trail runners like me are accustomed to twisting, rocky trails, short, abrupt climbs, and close-in horizons. Climb-running to the top of Catalina the next morning, I gaze 1500 feet down to Avalon Harbor, then out to the limitless expanse of the mighty Pacific – this world is telescopically larger than the one I come from – cinema-like.

A filmmaker brought buffalos to the island for a movie in 1924 and left them there. They now roam freely on 42,000 acres of Nature Conservancy land, which in large part contains the 100k figure-eight island circuit.

As an eleven year old, I remember sitting in the back of a '56 Chevy, hearing the Four Preps sing, "Twenty-six miles across the sea, Santa Catalina is a-waitin' for me," not knowing this was a foretelling of my karma - that I was meant to go there to run decades later.

Something different comes to me deep into the 100k distance, in creeping darkness, cold wind, and driving rain. I think, "This is ridiculous. I could be in my cozy warm hotel room watching sports on TV." My other self replies, "I don't think so. This is precisely why you are here, remember? You want to BE the action, not watch the action."

The few 50k's and two 50 milers I've run have not taken me past the edge of normalcy – now, I pass willingly into untracked space. I recall Slavomir Rawicz's "*The Long Walk*," where he escapes from a Siberian prison and walks 4000 miles to India. If he endured months scavenging on the run, I can press on here in relative luxury. I'm not hurt. I'm not going to die. I've got water and orange slices in my pocket.

As the road starts its decline toward Avalon, I figure only an hour or so more. It's less cold off the windy ridge, but still pouring rain and blowing hard. I see a lone flashlight moving through the switchbacks below – I'm lit, too. I would be warm if I could move faster, but my body's sluggishness keeps me from generating warmth. Torrents of water gush across the trail. There's no longer any point in trying to avoid them. From the steep rocky banks on my right, chunks of earth and stones slide noisily down behind me. In the darkness I am more alert, and strangely, more calm.

Fourteen hours and change, the body thrashed, the mind willing – a breakthrough. This is new: always, until this moment, physical exhaustion would take my mind down with my body. Now, I'm enveloped in a lively consciousness that pulls my spent body with it. Thank you, Baz. Thank you, karma. When can I do it again?

The Magic's beckoning stays with me. I live the Magic, going deep in ultra runs. It comes when the body's weak complaining gives way to the soul's murmuring reassurances, "You will not die doing this… You will not die EVER."

———

There's another ultra on Catalina, called the Avalon Benefit. Karma drew me to a return engagement. I went there again to run, five years later.

AVALON 50 MILE RUN
January 14, 2006

Millions of stars and the full yellow moon followed me across the country to California. I was here on Catalina, many runs ago. I wait again in morning darkness, to start the 2006 Avalon 50 miler.

People travel three thousand miles, yet they're still in the same place. Some ultras are called "Self Transcendence" events. Revelation comes with ego loss, a gateway to feeling one with the total energy of the universe. Long distance running invites one to lose the drape of mortality, to straighten circular thinking, to live in the spaces between the noise.

That's why I'm here, still advancing in the transition from pusher to puller.

The mayor gives a one-minute speech no one listens to. A raven's territorial "quork" startles me. We move with a signal to begin. Flashlights sweep the ground. Within ten seconds, a runner, head down to see, dead flushes a signpost, put suddenly on his back.

I've chosen beautiful venues to run ultras – Vermont woods, Mt. Hood forest, Canada wilderness, Catalina. In trail running, look up and you'll trip on a rock or root, and fall. I've missed the beauty of these places, looking down. Then again, looking down there's the hurting signpost, or the fallen tree five feet above the trail that clothes lined a welt on me last summer in the Adirondacks. It's a contact sport if you can't find a way to slip into the beauty untouched. Observe, respect, move.

Ultrarunning's irony is that fitness obsession is narcissistic, yet it works to suppress the preoccupied self, toward selfless presence in unbound consciousness.

Accomplishing fifty miles in one bite, or a hundred miles if you like, requires months and years of practicing the long run. The long run takes you through the wall so many times the wall disappears. You learn that hydration, electrolytes, food, and body care make a running checklist. Often there's a soft patch in the 35 – 45 mile range where your body tries to tell you "Enough!" And your mind will tell it "Not so!" This is the point of departure. Knowing it's there, the seasoned ultrarunner comes back to find it again and again.

Awareness of breath cycles offers easiest access to this spirituality. The four-step breath cycle is for steady going, three-step cycle is up tempo, two-step cycle for maximum effort. You become absorbed in the tempo of breath cycles, displacing signals of discomfort from the body. Pain is good. It tends to dissolve artificial limits. Extreme pain is extremely good – felt many times it becomes ordinary, like reaching into your pocket for a boarding pass. It's a ticket to ride through time, beyond mortality.

We run in the dark for two hours. This event has 6500 feet of vertical, a lot of it in the first seven miles. Fast walking up a slope I face the low full yellow moon, my friend. I could be a root vegetable, right here.

Ravens have observed this annual migration of the curious running people for twenty-five years. Moving across the high hogback of Catalina, I see a pair of them not ten feet away; one the sentinel, one reclining in a rock. I have never seen a rock so comfortable. They sit smug in raven brain that we excursionists cannot fly, that we will soon be gone for another twelve months: "Clumsy pointless earthbound creatures; we pre-exist them."

Flight conditions develop seven hours later. I have moved through the point of departure, somewhere in the forties; slow jog, breath cycling up a gradual slope.

I am not tired; I am beyond tired. I am soaring, lifted in thermal energy, just here, like the raven gliding. This is the presence.

And it stays with you after you've finished - more and more with every long run, you are less and less tightly held by ego's cravings, lighter of foot and freer from the persistence of random thinking.

From mile 34 to mile 47 Catalina gives you its long uphill. Then the last 2½ miles pour down to Avalon, past eucalyptus, the mighty Pacific in view. Here I've got the mojo to run two-step breath cycles, quads brake-busting in gravity's pull. This energy gathers up a spent runner, reduced to walking. Now he runs immediately behind me through the last mile, as on a tether. We finish one second apart, or at the exact moment, if measured in eons.

For most of us these are not races, they are opportunities. People asking, "How was your race? What was your time?" don't understand, don't get it. That's OK. It's not a question of right or wrong, better or worse. That, too, misses it.

The ultimate ultrarunning event extends so far past the point of departure that it has no end. I'm already signed up for that one, just waiting for the raven's "quork."

Returning to "America" on the high speed ferry, I see dolphins easily matching its 34-knot speed, expressing their joy with full body leaps into the chill Pacific air. I imagine smiles on their faces, thinking they may never come back down.

———

I train in Boston. My usual 10 mile run takes me on the Boston Marathon course, out and back, up Heartbreak Hill. On quiet mornings I imagine 111 years of surging lead pack champions, cresting to see the Prudential building six miles distant – the finish. Arriving there, they just keep going.

The Magic lurks. I've worked for years to coax it, not knowing when it might come to me, but more and more wanting it. I still don't know its secrets, but I can say, now it is more often with me.

———

ORIGINS

My last name, Bouscaren, is French. My mother was Scots-Irish, named McNulty. Both sets of forebears came to the United States in the middle of the 19th century: the Bouscarens via Guadeloupe, where they had fled to escape political persecution, the McNultys driven by hardship of the Irish Potato Famine. Bouscarens and McNultys were Catholic; born so, I was too.

Leaving college during World War Two to join the Marines, my Dad became a bomber pilot in the Pacific theater, fighting Japan. I was born in San Francisco, after the War, where Dad earned a Ph.D. in political science and began his career as a college professor.

My brother Tony is two years older than I am, and my brother Joe is ten years younger. Taking Dad's cue on sports and competition, we joined baseball and football teams, played imaginary big-league games with pebbles as balls and sticks as bats, and backyard touch football until dark or when Mom called us in for dinner. We lived in Wisconsin, watched the Milwaukee Braves, and followed the Green Bay Packers. When we moved to Syracuse, we took to skiing.

I ski raced through college, winning the division two Eastern downhill championship race in 1969. I played middle linebacker on a Yale football team that took two consecutive Ivy League championships with sixteen straight wins, and received All-Ivy honors my senior year.

I thought I was a stud; I was wrong. I had so much to learn, and so much to unlearn. I joined the Navy to avoid the draft, coming out aimless after two years, went to business school for an M.B.A., started work as a grain merchandiser in the Midwest, then quit and went to Boston, where I decided to settle. With luck, I shifted jobs from grain trader to bond trader to investment advisor, in a few short years.

———

RUN TO LIVE; LIVE TO RUN

My first long distance event was the American Birkebeiner, a 30+ mile cross-country ski race in Wisconsin. I was thirty years old, living in a woodsy setting near Boston. Abundant winter snow allowed me to ski out from my house into the surrounding woods, where I followed circuitous trails for miles, in stunning, wondrous silence. I sensed I could find my place in this world, that nature would share its secrets with me, if I continued these excursions.

Wantonly egotistic, I thought people did not understand me, or give me what I thought I deserved. In my formative years, so much was freely given to me that I developed expectations of privilege. I didn't care about much because I hadn't worked hard enough or made commitments deep enough to care. I avoided commitments, out of fear that I might lose the subjects of my attention – relationships especially. I was unhappy and didn't know why, but if I went for a run, I always came back feeling better.

I ran the Boston Marathon, my first, one year after the "Birkie." I remember hearing Bill Rodgers' winning finish on a spectator's radio, as I passed through mile sixteen, with ten more to go. I remember struggling up Heartbreak Hill alongside a tall, pale, middle aged woman, thinking, "How can I let a woman like this run with me? I'm a damn football star, strong as a moose, and this mom in a purple top is matching me, challenging me to keep up with her. Am I some kind of weakling?" For me, understanding "What is strength?" would come much later.

Whatever - all I knew was that running made me feel good about myself, especially when other things that I did, didn't. The big plusses: I married Deedie, my best friend and partner, and we were blessed with three wonderful girls. Good luck took me into the world of investment management, and I landed a high-paying job on Wall Street. The huge minus: I was a miserable alcoholic. By good fortune, my wife and employer intervened to stop me, separately and simultaneously, and it worked. The year that I quit drinking, I ran Boston again; my second marathon, thirteen years after the first. I remember fighting through blisters, dehydration and hyperthermia in the final miles, all consequences of not knowing how to prevent them. I willed myself to the finish, knowing my family waited to see me there. There's power in that.

My fastest marathon time was Ocean State, the third one, in three hours and thirty-four minutes, at the age of forty-six. Wild energy drove me. After eight years in New York, we had decided to move back to Boston, but I had not yet resigned from my Wall Street job, or found another one, nor had we put the house up for sale or found schools for the girls to attend. Mentally, I was in a space like at the start of a sprint, where you've heard the gun go off but haven't yet physically reacted to it: pent up angst drove me to that record marathon finish. I thought, "If I really hammer this one, it will give me the strength to deal effectively with my life's unfinished business." And it did.

I ran these marathons to affirm myself and to generate more drive and confidence in the real world, where social inadequacies continued to haunt me. If I could not "work a crowd" or remember names, these did not diminish my self-esteem as much as they might, since I could now claim to be a marathon runner.

———

IT'S A LONG WAY UP THE LEARNING CURVE

WATER

Training for Ocean State, I tell a friend I finished a nineteen mile run, but felt hot and weak near the end of it. He asks, "Did you drink enough water?" "Water?" I reply, "I didn't have any water." In my sports experience, taking water was never thought essential. In the 1960's we ate steak and eggs before football games; to drink water during the game was considered a mild form of surrender. You could almost hear the coaches thinking, "Aren't you guys tough enough to skip the water?"

Now in the 1990's, I began to include water as part of my long runs, driving out beforehand and placing plastic water bottles behind bushes and trees along my intended route. While running Fred's marathon in Fitchburg, Massachusetts, I hid water bottles behind various trees so well that I couldn't find any of them. For this ingenuity, dehydration slowed me through the final miles. And in winter training runs my hidden water bottles would sometimes freeze before I got to them. So I knew to have water, but couldn't always access it.

About the same time that I understood water is essential when running a marathon, I also learned that you can't always count on finding it along the course, even when people tell you it's going to be there. During the Nantucket Marathon in 1998, the water station promised at mile 14 was simply not there, nor any from miles 15 through 22. On that day, dehydration combined with cold damp weather, putting hypothermia deep enough into me that I was seeing double near the end. After that, I got a CamelBak to be sure I'd have water when I wanted it.

COTTON

All through organized sports I wore cotton shirts, so naturally, I wore them running. When cotton absorbs moisture from perspiration, it stays in the fabric; if the day turns cooler, wet cotton clothing will chill you. I got chilled regularly for years, in training runs and in marathons until I learned to wear synthetic, wicking materials that are far more comfortable in varying conditions. The same goes for socks. If you're new to long distance running, try the new generation fabrics – they will let you run unimpeded.

Before, I'd be ten miles out, wearing a cotton sweatshirt on a thirty degree afternoon in sleeting conditions, trying to locate my hidden (now frozen) water bottle: "Brrr, I'm parched and freezing. Now where'd I put that damn water - I swear I left it right here in this bush, next to that signpost." Now, in similar nasty conditions, I glide past that same signpost in layered comfort, while sipping from my CamelBak, worn inside to keep from freezing.

BEYOND THE MARATHON

My marathon finishes (now eight) were getting slower. The lore has it that middle-aged people lose three per cent of their speed every year. I began to doubt I could finish the next marathon under four hours. I thought, "If I can't break four hours, I'll be a failure." Age imposes limits. I can be stubborn, but I won't beat myself up if the challenge is unrealistic. From all I'd read about training, I knew I could practice running intervals or go to the track and work on speed, but I also recognized there would be a much higher chance of injury if I tried that. I began to think of objectives not so time driven, so that I could run long distance events and still be happy with the results.

I needed a rule change. It came to me on Stan Jensen's Run100's website, where I read, "In ultrarunning, the last finisher is the slowest winner". I learned the average age in a typical event is mid-forties. Ultrarunners celebrate that they can complete the distance, more than how long it takes them to do it. "To hell with four hour marathons," I thought. " Ultrarunning is for me."

―――

FIRST 50K – "SYBIL"
April 24, 1999

(see page 9)

The Sybil Ludington 50k comes every April, convenient to anyone living in the New York/New England area. It's named after a Colonial era girl who rode her horse around the territory north of New York City, shouting, "The British are coming," just like Paul Revere. There's a statue of Sybil in the park near the finish. The course is a scenic country road loop; the event is low key. I remember passing through mile 26.2 (marathon distance), and continuing through the next five miles amazed that I could go on at all, thinking after the finish, "Fifty kilometers isn't so hard, if you just slow down a little." Perfect – I was slowing down anyway.

SLOUGH OF DESPOND 50K
October 9, 1999

Six months later, I went to Ontario for the Slough of Despond 50k, on the Bruce Peninsula near Lake Huron and the town of Wiarton. There, an eight foot statue of a groundhog named Wiarton Willie, the town mascot, graces a small park overlooking the lake. Why else except to run, would I ever be in a place like this?

Slough of Despond 50k runners
walk to the start.

Now discontinued, the Slough of Despond 50k included a stretch on the Bruce Trail, my first exposure to trail running. I discovered you have to be careful where you plant your feet if you want to stay vertical. The running stride is irregular, guided by how you react to rocks, roots, and puddles in the track. Trail running is multi-dimensional; compared to road running, it's more entertaining and slower. Near the finish, as I closed on two runners ahead of me, squinting to focus better, I saw there was in fact only one – that's a symptom of electrolyte depletion, but I didn't know it then.

With a group of finishers in the motel waiting turns for a shower, I heard one of them say, "There used to be a 50 miler here along with this 50k. That extra nineteen miles is a long way to go, after you've done the first thirty-one."

ELECTROLYTES

After you've run three hours or so, your body's store of essential electrolytes, especially sodium and potassium, gets used up. If you want to go on happily, you'll need to put more electrolytes into your system. Electrolyte pills can be found in running stores or online, and they're as important to the ultrarunner as water and not wearing cotton. So I got bottle of salt pills and thought I'd try a 50 miler.

———

CHAPTER TWO: MOVING UP

There's discussion among purists whether 50k's should even be considered ultramarathons, since they're much closer to marathon distance than the step up to 50 miles. No question that to train for a 50 mile event you have to pile on more training mileage than for a 50k.

DISTANCE TRAINING

I followed a well recognized formula when starting out in the marathon distance: begin with weekly mileage in the 20-30 range, including one day where you go longer than the others, say, starting at 6 to 8 miles. Every week or every other week, add 1 mile to the long run, and 1-2 miles to the weekly total until you're in the 40 mile per week range with a long run of 17-19 miles. You then finish the training cycle, prior to the essential two week taper, by running at least three consecutive weeks in the low to mid-40's, including two 20 mile long runs on either end of a 16-18 mile long run in the middle. That takes from 14 to 20 weeks, including the taper, where you cut your maximum weekly mileage two weeks before the marathon in half, and in the final week by one-third; say, just 14 miles in the last week, with at least two full days of rest before the event itself. I call this program "Cow to Panther" to describe how your physical condition and self-confidence will change – guaranteed. You will be ready for the marathon distance and optimistic that you will be able to run 26.2 miles without a hitch, provided you rate your pace in the first 13 miles consistent with your long run training pace.

Training for the 50k distance is easier if you've been through marathon training cycles a few times. Just increase total weekly mileage and work in back-to-back longer runs; say, starting with 13 milers on consecutive days. This practice will increase endurance and is the key component of ultrarunning training. Get into the 50 mile per week range, with back-to-back long runs one weekend, then a single long run of at least 25 miles the following weekend, then back-to-back the next. Try to make at least three consecutive 50 mile weeks, then taper for 2-3 weeks in the same manner as a marathon taper. Never think you need to run in the few days prior to an event to stay in condition; believe me, you are already trained up, and you'll need the rest.

Running fifty miles takes time; you will be on your feet for the better part of a full day, and training for the first 50 miler should include a lot of time on your feet in addition to running. Apply the 50k training regimen, with back-to-back runs of 20 miles each at least three times, and single long runs in the 25-30 mile range. You don't have to exceed 50+ mile weeks, but you do need to make those long back-to-backs. Take more full days of rest – even 3-4 days a week – while putting in longer short runs on training days. A typical cycle: Monday off; Tuesday 10 miles; Wednesday off; Thursday 10 miles; Friday off; Saturday 30 miles; Sunday, Monday off; Tuesday 10 miles; Wednesday off; Thursday 5 miles; Friday off; Saturday

20 miles; Sunday 20 miles; Monday off, and so on. On long run days, eat a nutritious meal within 40 minutes after finishing the run, rest an hour or two, then go for a long walk or an easy bike ride, to make an 8-12 hour day of total activity, the same amount of time it will take you to finish the 50 mile run.

———

BULL RUN 50 MILER - VIRGIN NO LONGER
April 15, 2000

The Bull Run Run 50 miler is an April event in Manassas, Virginia, on the Bull Run-Occoquon Trail, within the 4000 acre park maintained by the Northern Virginia Regional Park Authority. Hosted by the friendly folks of the Virginia Happy Trails Running Club, Bull Run is a must do – and my first 50 miler.

I learned about Bull Run on the internet, picking up the lore of ultrarunning from various websites, reading training tips and first hand accounts by experienced ultrarunners. I prepared for it with two 50k road events six months apart and some intense training to reach peak conditioning in the weeks immediately prior. This would be a leap of faith. I moved with hard training from doubt, to hope, to determination that I could do it. By race day, I was ready.

Arriving Friday afternoon for the Saturday morning event, I checked into a hotel in Manassas and went directly to the Hemlock Campsite to register and join in on the pre-run pasta feed. There, I saw some of the "gods" I'd taken advice and inspiration from on the web, to ramp up my training over the past few months. I met others deep in the ultra culture as well – the nicest and most genuine slice of life I've ever encountered. I sat next to Gary Knipling. When I asked him about leaving a bag drop (containing things I might need during the run, like socks, snacks, energy powder, etc.) at the half-way point, he said Bull Run wasn't set up for that. "Since this is your first 50 miler, you must be anxious," Gary added. "Why don't you ask Stan and Marge if they would help? They are running the aid stations at mile 24.5 and mile 40." I introduced myself to them, and without hesitation, Stan got up from his dinner and took me out into parking lot to point out his van, under which he said I could leave my drop bag. He'd make sure it would be there at his aid station.

In a casual way, Stan told me Marge had just set her personal best in a 100 mile run the previous week. Many people I met at Bull Run have run 100's, and much of the conversation during the early part of the run itself (before the energy to talk so much is spent) involved past ultras completed or future plans for such. For me, this crowd is generally at a much higher level of running accomplishment than I've ever witnessed (including the eight marathons I'd run and the two 50 k's); for me, this is a crowd of running "gods."

Saturday morning at 5:30: I'm walking in the dark under light rain toward the Hemlock mess hall, hoping that a couple more cups of coffee will give me just a bit more energy. Soon I toe the line, and with a simple "GO!" from race director (or, RD), Scott Mills, runners bump off in single file into the woods, for what I can only imagine lies ahead.

Bull Run runners leave drop bags at the
Hemlock Overlook start/finish area.

Since I've never before run long on a trail, and since the "gods" have told me Bull Run is a good first trail run, I expect it will be like the many road runs I've completed over the years. Not so. Within the first two miles there are stream crossings, rock fields, fallen logs, and only a few places to run freely.

The training advice I've studied includes the necessity of walking, say, one minute for every five minutes of running, to conserve energy. I plan to run/walk from early on, but this single file obstacle course won't offer the opportunity to control when to walk or run. In the cliché of sport, "The opposition determines the pace of play." When my file of runners finally emerges onto a straight and open path, there's slippery mud, and roots and rocks underfoot, which call for eye attention (on roads, one can look ahead, or marvel at the sky, or sightsee). I fall down three times in the first 14 miles, each time avoiding a face plant with a double straight-arm catch of the ground; it goes like this: left foot plants, right foot strides ahead, left toe catches a root, immobilizing left foot while the rest of self propels forward. From these falls I feel my ankle muscles tearing slightly. Trail runners, I gather, pick up their feet more, while road runners can indulge in a low striding shuffle, if it suits them.

The mile 15.5 aid station is also the start location, where many people have left drop bags. I change socks (feet are already wet) and grab some gorp in a zip-lock bag, leave my cap (drenched) in exchange for a bandana (I don't realize how useful it will be), and move out. I set my mind simply into making Stan and Marge's 24.5 mile aid station, where I can take good measure of my condition, to compare how I feel there to the many 25 mile training runs I've done to get ready for this.

This is the "Mother Duck" part. I catch up to a female runner with a following of runners close behind, all chatting actively. For me, chatting and running are like walking and chewing gum for the physically challenged – I'm sort of a brief comment guy. If there's any talk at all, it's more like, "Way to go" or "Good job," so both the catching up and the chatter make me want to pass them, to quieter ground, as it were. This is when I take a fourth fall, tripping on a branch hidden in the leaves on the edge of the single track. Again, no big deal, the same straight-arm catch and same leg muscle pull, except this time I get the "double toe jam" where both feet slam immovable objects, causing big time toe pain and no small embarrassment, in close view of the file of "ducks" chattering alongside me. Long distance running's great pleasure comes when your mind roams freely into the realm of the unconscious, hoisting from the depths of memory and imagination so many interesting "deep sea creatures" for consideration. After I recover from the stumble and move ahead into the more manageable solitude of the trail, I check out my condition: ankle is OK but needs another ibuprofen. I also take another 500mg salt tab, slurp some liquid energy mix from my CamelBak, and see I'm almost at the mile 24.5 aid station and refreshment. Then, memory and imagination fish out the thought, "That was the same woman I passed miles ago, and I fell that time, too!" Now the Mother Duck looms Freudian: in his life, Mike wants to break free of the controlling female but stumbles trying to do so. Mike could fall in line behind her, like the other ducks (who are mere followers), but Mike's fate is to pursue true independence (and nearly break his ankle attempting it). How hard it is for Mike to find true independence; or worse, possibly Mike is destined never to find it! Stumble on, wandering mind!

The "Do Loop," which has garnered much fanfare from race organizers and participants, starts in mile 32. I figure it's probably just harder; steeper hills, bigger streams, more obstacles underfoot, and I'm right. Since my longest run to date has been 31 miles, I'm in uncharted territory now; still, all body parts are moving adequately, and I'm able to maintain relentless forward progress. The more tired I get, the more I have to focus on the mechanics of foot placement and hydration, now wiping my face with the bandana for simple and renewing relief, to clean off salt and sweat and dust. "This is the stuff of ultramarathoners" I think. "Deep in the woods, into the mile 30's, willing the corpus along (it will go so long as you keep it hydrated and fed). What a MAN I am!" Some new psychic energy puts more lift into my stride.

The aid station at mile 35 has grilled cheese sandwiches – mmm. Having sampled bananas, orange slices, potatoes, cantaloupe, fig newtons, gorp, pineapple, Gatorade, water, Mountain Dew, Coke, orange soda, some other electrolyte drink, and a couple of M&M's, I'm struck that every different taste makes a special treat.

Getting to mile 40 from 35 is key. The concentration and will needed to avoid stumbling, to go down the ravines and walk up the other side, to start running again when the trail flattens out – all reach near maximum. At one stream crossing, while greeting and passing an older guy with a cheerful pleasantry, I catch up to a woman runner. She says in exasperation, "My legs don't do stream crossings anymore," and plunges ankle deep, while I gingerly skip from rock top to rock top (dry) to the other side. Just that little sense of advantage helps me think I'm doing comparatively well, lifting my spirits yet again. I realize the energy from here on out would be the fumy stuff of my imagination and my will. Right here, I believe there is no doubt I will finish.

There's Marge (of 100 mile fame) at the mile 40 aid station. Ordinary chicken soup has never tasted so good. I rationalize, 10 miles isn't so much more - just get to the next aid station – mile 44.5. I drop my CamelBak at mile 40 to lighten my load for the final stretch.

My back and leg are cramping a bit, so I walk briefly to relax the muscles, then resume running. Coming to a log bridge over the mud-slop, I slip sideways, catching myself with a quick, reactionary stabilizing move that cramps my right side so tightly I have to walk again until the muscles relax.

I come back through soccer fields around 4 p.m., the same soccer fields I crossed from the other direction about 11 a.m., only now there are different teams and players and parents and dogs, but still the same Dad voice bellowing: "SHOOT" to some intimidated son or daughter. I think, "Hey, Dad - why don't you play your own game?"

Going down a ravine after mile 44.5, I figure three things: there are only five miles left (even couch potatoes can run five miles), orange slices really do taste better after you've been running for almost 10 hours, and, most importantly, "WATER IS SMARTER THAN PEOPLE."

Why water is smarter than people: unlike people, who may trip and stumble on obstacles in the trail, water always takes the way of least resistance. If I were water, I would never have fallen or misstepped or banged three or four toenails into terminal purple loss. Beginning now in this ravine and for the rest of the run, I'm going to run like water.

On the Bull Run website there's a picture of the "ladder steps," leading to the final half mile. I picture seeing them, knowing that they will yield to the green grass field, the gravel road, and the finish. But first the trail turns up and out of the river way, to higher ground. By my watch I figure the turn should be just around the bend, just around the bend ... but there are only more rock fields and stream crossings. A fellow 200 yards behind starts yelling, "Where's the turn - did you miss it?" I fear that after nearly 50 miles of running, I might now be lost. Then just around the bend I see ladder steps. Away, doubt! As much as I really, really want to run up these steps, all I can do is walk them carefully to avoid the shuddering toe jam, thus methodically cresting the hill onto the green grassy field. It's just a quick lope to the finish. Scott Mills greets me with a handshake and congratulations

- the most fulfilling 10 hours 43 minutes of continuous effort I've ever endured to this point.

People ask, "Why do you run 50 miles?" I knew before, it was to test the limits of will against physical fatigue, to probe deeper wanderings of memory and imagination, to make the body's complaints yield to a stronger power. But I found a new reason today; for one glorious stretch of time, I too was able to run with the "gods".

––––––

RAMP IT

Behavioral psychologists have learned by studying brain chemistry that it's not unusual for people to inflict pain on themselves; it brings feelings of deservedness, for instance. I proudly went home after Bull Run with a badly swollen ankle from all the root-banging, bruised toes with broken nails, and a sore back. Football experience had me thinking physical damage should be an expected consequence of something as unimaginable as running 50 miles. Hard-wired Catholic teaching had me thinking that suffering on earth brings eternal reward. That's a little twisted, but I wanted more of it.

My toes healed before I went to New Jersey for the Garden State 50 miler in September, 2000. As we rode the bus to the start, a fellow asked me, "How

many ultramarathons like this do you run in a year?"
Truth be told, this was my second 50 miler EVER,
but I told him, "Two," not wanting to show what a
rookie I was (the rationalization: "Well, I HAVE run
two events in each of the past three years, except
they were marathons twice, and 50k's once."). I was a
self-conscious beginner; in conditioned reluctance to
tell the truth about myself, I acted the pretender, still
fooling myself, still uncomfortable in my own skin.

On Wall Street and elsewhere, many people develop a
sense of identity through their work. Self-importance
for them comes out of achievement, recognition
among peers, and money. The office, the title, the
fawning employees: these elevate the sense of self
worth – artificially, it seemed to me. I was one of
them, yet I never felt comfortable thinking of myself
that way. I pictured everyone suddenly placed far
out in the harshness of nature – who would be
comfortable when comfort could not be bought?
Dropped naked in the wild, who would know how to
survive? I wanted to be the one who knew how to
survive, when all the trappings of convenience and
self-importance were of no practical use. But I was
among the helpless ones myself, standing there in
that imaginary wilderness, not really knowing how to
be self-sufficient. Long distance running whispered
it might hold the key to help me become the person
I wanted to be, to help me stop pretending to be the
person that I wasn't.

———

MOUNT HOOD PCT 50 MILE TRAIL RUN
August 11, 2001

Training in summer heat is a first for me. This time, I use marathons for long training runs, including the Sherwood, R.I. road marathon in May, and the Nipmuck trail marathon in June. One day toward the end of June, I run 32 miles in Craftsbury, Vt., in 80 degree heat, for my final long training run, hassled by noxious insect repellent and the methane fog of cow shit coming from nearby dairy farms. In all of these runs I feel mild nausea near the finish, probably due to insufficient hydration. I try Succeed electrolyte caps, replacing the simpler salt tabs I've used previously and experiment with different energy replacement mixes in the CamelBak. The 3rd annual Mt Hood PCT 50 miler looks to offer heat, moderate altitude, and spectacular scenery – new challenges in a beautiful setting.

I fly from Boston to Portland on Thursday, to check out the course and the conditions. Like many East coast provincials, I didn't know the Pacific Coast Trail (Western counterpart to our Appalachian Trail) stretches 2650 miles from California to Washington's Cascade mountains and is one of the premier hiking destinations in the world. I stay in the town of Government Camp, which caters to the summer skiers on Mount Hood.

It's 49 degrees Friday morning and over 90 by mid-afternoon, with the forecast the same for Saturday. I drive in morning darkness to the start near Timothy Lake and see that I'll need a flashlight for the optional 5:30 a.m. start (6:30 is the regular start, but that would make a hotter day of running). I drive up to the half-way turnaround point at Timberline Lodge, altitude 6000 feet, and sniff the thinner air. No problem, I hope. Next, a huge huckleberry pancake breakfast, then back to the room for final preparations.

I plan to have one drop bag at mile 25 (event support people take drop bags to designated aid stations) with a change of socks, shirt, 3 packs of gu, and 3 bottles with Accelerade powder in measures for 10 miles, 5 miles, and 10 miles to match aid station locations where I can use their water and put the mix into my CamelBak as needed. For the first 25 miles, I have a 24 oz. mix in the camelback, gu, and 2 bottles carried in the rear webbing. People advise getting 50% of your nutrition from liquid and 50% from solids. As the temperature rises into the 90's, I make a final realistic estimate of my expected completion time: 11 hours. Bull Run was 10:43, and Garden State 9:42, but I figure with the heat and possible altitude issues, I should scale back expectations and run more slowly to avoid a dreaded bonk (energy loss from insufficient fuel consumption) or DNF (Did Not Finish).

Six of us take the early Saturday start option (43 would start an hour later), and with little fanfare, move out onto the trail at 5:30. The first 19 miles are straightforward: hold back a little, drink and pee a lot (anywhere in the woods will do), and conserve energy.

Mt. Hood PCT runners check their watches at
the 6:30 a.m. start

I'm determined not to fall down during this run. At
Bull Run, I ate dirt 6-8 times, and at the Nipmuck,
rocks tripped me down even more (There, people
wear hand/wrist protectors, which I'd not seen before
in a trail run). Unlike hockey players, who must look
UP to avoid getting decked, trail runners have to
look DOWN to avoid getting decked. This presents
conflict to one inspired by the magnificent beauty of
Mt. Hood in its snow-covered, 11,239 foot majesty. In
hour two of the run, as the mighty mountain comes
into view, pow! Rocks underfoot catch my toe, and
I stumble, not quite falling. I take this as a wake up
call, like a boxer catching an unseen jab from his
opponent – better get more focused, and better
look down!

I stay vertical for about four hours before tripping
in mile 22 when distracted by three day hikers at a
road crossing. Approaching horizontal, I manage
a fingertip save, avoiding body contact with the
ground: "No knock-down, only a slip," I think. Diving
shoulder rolls, wrenched knee spin-downs, face plants

– those would be legitimate knock-downs. My vertical streak stays alive.

Beyond the Barlow Pass aid station at mile 19, the trail climbs 2000 feet to the turnaround on Mt. Hood at Timberline. Having seen pictures of the sand fields above the tree line on the event website, I'm eager to see this mile high beach area. As I work through the sand, enjoying the sweet smell and purple beauty of the wildflowers (lupine), a fellow named Pierce Cornelius passes me. Later, I see he's bettered my finishing time by 45 minutes, and he's 70 years old – amazing!

At the mile 25 (Timberline Lodge) turnaround, I spend a few extra minutes to wash the dust off my feet, then traverse back through the sand fields – much easier going down. The day is perfectly clear with Mt. Hood's unmatched beauty over my left shoulder and the sound of gushing water from the snow melt bringing the scene alive. Then back into the woods, which are hotter and dustier than when I came up.

Reaching the Wapinitia Pass/ Hwy 26 aid station at mile 35.5, I'm hot and sense the dreaded bonk creeping into me. I take time for watermelon, bananas, cantaloupe, pretzels, and ice water, topped with Succeed and ibuprofen. "Have to slow down for a while," I think, "fourteen miles to go: just walk a little more, and drink, drink, drink to chase the bonk away."

I resume a jog/shuffle and right away, pow! The rocks go after the middle toe on my right foot. Like a fighter whose eye has been closed by repeated blows, now unable to see the punches thrown at him, I sense the rocks want to knock me down with repeated shots to the same toe. The more I try to protect it, the more I bang it. Another people distraction behind me, and, POW !! The rocks launch me forward. To avoid a mouthful of trail dirt, I make a full contact, skinning hand save, and have to count it as a legitimate knock-down. Rocks one; Mike zero.

In the context of British writer Lord Byron's famous "Truth is stranger than fiction," these Mt. Hood rocks seem alive, as much as the gushing snowmelt. Lord Byron once swam the Hellespont despite his club foot handicap – the truth of his life being more outlandish than the fiction of his work. Similar odd confusion is at work here.

Now in the 9th or 10th hour, with the temperature in the 90's, I consider the fine line between truth and fiction. Conclusively, I see that truth comes out of a strong imagination, while fiction is mostly what people think when they're not really thinking. Consider the OREGON GAZE. This is a phenomenon observed by exhausted ultrarunners who pass day hikers on the PCT. The hiker, appearing fresh and hearty, makes eye contact with the ultrarunner – deep eye contact – as if to affirm an already decided upon fiction. So in the question posed, "Are you alright?" she betrays her fictional impression that I'm not. My reply: "Of course I'm all right; can't you SEE?"

With 3 miles to go, the trail gets more rocky and dusty. Since I've put more cold water onto my head than into my stomach, I'm dry and empty. This is the good part, the moment ultrarunners of all abilities look forward to: "How am I going to dig a little deeper to keep myself going?" I scream silently: "You didn't come all the way out here to walk, did you? Get it in gear, or you'll regret it!" I struggle to shuffle forward. Soon a passerby tells me it's only twenty minutes to the road.

Encouraged, I will myself on. Finally, as I work out of the woods, it's just a quarter mile to that wonderful "Finish" banner. Beautiful people who have already finished cheer and clap as I grind to a stop. Shortly, I'm one of those cheering for subsequent finishers, studying their expressions as I sit, dazed.

My finishing time is 10:55, with nearly even 25 mile splits. This result, so close to my expectations, shows that detailed imaging before an ultra event increases the chances of a satisfying result. In past runs, I'd done all the legwork and proper tapering, only to find that during the event my logistics were not thought out well enough, leading to time consuming complications. Now I know to plan ahead, allow a little slack time, and never underestimate the challenge.

Mt. Hood's wild beauty seems to homogenize truth and fiction. The fictional view at first seems very real; my impression that rocks jump, or what's behind the OREGON GAZE, for instance. Yet when I'm done, sitting there baking in 90 degree heat after this 50 mile run, truth emerges: I'm able to leave a little more of my fictional self behind and take a little more of my real self back home.

CHAPTER THREE: MIDDLE GROUND

Into my third year of ultrarunning, I'd reached a consistently higher level of fitness. By late summer 2001 I'd run a 50k, a 100k, a road marathon, a trail marathon, 50 miles at Mt. Hood, and was still hungry for more. People I'd met and read about seemed to have no problem coping with even more ambitious schedules. Both recovery after long distance events and new training cycles to reach peak conditioning took less time than in the year before, and the year before that.

I followed internet training advice, taking care not to over-train or push so hard during an event that I would risk serious injury. I read Tim Noakes' *The Lore of Running*, Jim Shapiro's *Meditations from the Breakdown Lane: Running Across America*, and other stories describing how people are able to accomplish unthinkable feats. The more events I finished, the easier they became. I decided the health benefits of this practice were so compelling that I would continue to ramp up my event calendar, while putting still more emphasis on nutrition, rest, and listening to my body's responses to what I was doing with it. I learned to know the difference between pushing hard for better conditioning and pushing myself into sickness or injury. My problems were brief: hamstring, calf, or knee issues – all remedied with several days' rest – and a few upper respiratory setbacks from running in severe winter cold.

Later in 2001, I ran the Clarence De Mar and Hartford fall marathons two weeks apart, then the inaugural Stone Cat Ale 50 miler here in Massachusetts, in early November, for a total of eight events in eleven months. Famous Alaskan musher Norman Vaughan's advice, "Dream big, and dare to fail" became my guiding principle. With the approaching year end holiday season offering some down time, I began plan for the 2002 campaign.

Jim "Gilly" Gilford – ultrarunner and Coach of Gil's Athletic Club, home to the Stone Cat Ale 50 miler, the Mother's Day 6 hour, and the turn of the year Fat Ass 50k.

IN CONTROL, OUT OF CONTROL

"Feel-good" carries risk, too. Though I indulged in persuasive, positive feedback from running ultra events and training for them, I recognized this increasing time commitment put stress on my marriage and family life. Not a runner, my wife Deedie told me (again and again) my new time allocation was taking away from time I owed our relationship, our family, and our social life. She had a point. I was like the dog that tries simultaneously to hold multiple objects in its mouth, but cannot manage – dropping one, hastily picking it up, then dropping another. I could not drop what was so dear to me. I owed Deedie my life: she saved me from the fate of terminal alcoholism when I was 44 years old. She told me I had to choose between her with our children or the bottle. I answered with the most important decision I have ever made: to lose the bottle and keep the family. Without Deedie, I'd probably be dead by now. Also, I had a full time job. How could I manage to keep running like this?

For me, running was more than just exercise and adventure. It was where I went to sort things out; to get in touch with myself; to cleanse my spirit; to give me strength to be a better husband, father, and friend. Running opened my way to happier living. I depended on it.

We talked. We agreed that family was more important than anything else, that we had to renew our commitment to keep ourselves together. I tried to explain that my sense of self was shifting from the blustery cocksure Wall Street persona to one being shaped with help from these ultra runs. I told her I wasn't sure where it was going, but I sensed that it was right for me, and necessary. I felt myself changing, but she was holding constant. She had social needs that I did not feel so keenly. I craved my alone time. Our commitment was tense. I trained every week between five and twelve hours, depending on what the next event required. Given how important running was to me, this did not seem unbalanced or excessive. She spent an equivalent amount of time playing tennis and practicing yoga. She wanted more of my time. I tried to create more time by shortening transitions, and by eliminating minutes wasted just shuffling around, unfocused; five minute showers, getting dressed in three minutes, being on time for everything, always. I've probably waited about five thousand hours for her to "get ready." So who was squandering time? Couldn't she wait for me? Yeah, I know; it was "apples and oranges."

Our two older girls, Chloe and Lila, were becoming more self-sufficient, now driving cars and close to high school graduation; and our third, Maggie, was a sixth grader. Already in my fifties, I felt strongly compelled to listen and act on the urgings of my inner voice, so on my death bed I wouldn't regret not having at least tried to fulfill my dreams or might possibly find myself closer to accepting whatever comes next. Deedie and I struggled to cope with our differences and our inevitably changing life, still trusting in our deeply shared commitment to each other, to our children, and to our future together. At times, we were physically close but mentally distant. She did not understand why running was so important to me; I didn't think it fair for her to claim my running time for herself.

I kept thinking, "Longer is better." I read personal accounts of 100 mile runs posted on the Run100's website and the inspirational, "You're better than you think you are and you can do more than you think you can," from Ken Chlouber's pre- Leadville 100 mile event speech. On dark cold winter mornings when bad weather kept me inside, I drank coffee and dreamed of some day running 100 miles myself for the first time. I thought it would be the ultimate rite of passage, proving my legitimacy as an ultrarunner. Running Stone Cat, I chatted with Ray Mount, who told me of his Vermont 100 and Western States 100 mile experiences. Ray and I contested for 50 miles that day in an undeclared race to the finish. He won, but I wasn't far behind – close enough for me to think Ken Chlouber could be right.

To this point I'd run five events 50 miles or longer and figured if I was going to attempt a 100 mile run, I should try the 100k distance again. There are few events with distances between 100k and 100 miles, so gaining familiarity with the very long run experience meant more 100k's for me. I chose the Withlacoochee 100k near Tampa, a paved rails-to-trails layout. After a relatively slow outing at Mt. Hood, I wanted to prove a faster long distance pace. Withlacoochee would give me the chance to set a personal best 100k time, give my trail battered toes a reprieve, and for the second time, take me to an ultra finish just 38 miles short of 100.

_____

WITHLACOOCHEE 100K
February 9, 2002

The 2002 Rails to Trails event went off in near perfect conditions. I began checking the weather forecast ten days in advance, and it's 85 degrees the week before – a swollen toed, many blistered possibility on the sun-hot asphalt. People planning a February trip to Florida would normally be disappointed to wake up the first day there to overcast, drizzly conditions, but not us twenty odd starters, shaking our legs before the 6 a.m. start – these are good conditions for a 62 mile run!

I'm an ultra internet junkie, indebted to Stan Jensen, Kevin Sayres, Don Allison, David Horton, and others who have taught me so much about ultrarunning, from this resource. I read their ultra reports, trying further to understand the Magic and how to catch it in the ultras that I run. John Dodds and John Prohira are especially gifted in describing the feeling of going deep, in its stress and in its humor. And there are so many others who have been there, whose stories inspire my 3:50 a.m. wake-ups for those 10 mile training runs on weekdays before work, and the long runs on weekends.

The zone is serendipitous. Last fall, while watching Chris Matthews'"Hardball," I saw Rob Schultheis talking about Pathans, their caves, and the topography of Afghanistan. There was something in his eyes saying, "Come with me." I sent for his book *Night Letters*, but that wasn't it. In his other books, *Bone Games*, *Fool's Gold*, and *The Hidden West*, he relates his quest for the vision, the near-satori, the out of body experience we begin to feel when we run ultras.

Fool's Gold is about Telluride, the San Juans, Hardrock 100 ground (rated toughest of them all). It led me to Bob Boeder's *Hardrock Fever*, which he autographed for me with "To Mike – Keep the faith. Never give up." I waited to read Bob's book on the flight to Tampa, hoping it would help me peak emotionally for Withlacoochee. Bob didn't let me down.

There's the pace: you want to conserve, but you want your best result. You want to go deeper than ever before, but not so deep that you can't come back again to run another day. On trail runs, hills determine the pace. On flat runs like Withlacoochee, going out too fast would be a fatal temptation. For lack of a better estimate, I take a conservative, hypothetical 50k road time, double it, then add 10-20% to arrive at a goal between 12 and 13 hours.

The rail bed is so straight that in the morning darkness, it looks as if we are running in a space left after the world has been cut in half. With the drizzle, I figure to go up tempo a bit to put time in the bank, in case it gets sunny and hot later. After about 35 minutes and 5k, it's still dark at the first aid station. Aid stations wait for runners every 5k to the 25k turnaround - a double out and back layout. Quick math in the head; let's see, 35 times five, add a little walking time after every aid station, that's a three hour lap, right at the edge of my imaginary envelope. Go there.

Many of the aid station volunteers are ultrarunners also, not failing to ask, "What can I get you?" as runners approach. This is funny to me: the question seems framed in the interest of not having to slow people down as they fly on to a WR, a PR, or the coveted gold winner's buckle. I'm working a 12 minute mile pace. Heck, I don't know what aid I want until I see what you have first, and it's all covered up to stay out of the drizzle. I have to lift and peek, spoiling precious seconds, tupperware tops wresting away any hope for fame and glory, har, har ! Fortified with a bit of banana or orange or pretzel, I walk about 100 yards to stretch out, before resuming the run. Repeat 20 times 'til done – seems simple enough.

I make 25k in just under three hours. Reload the CamelBak with Accelerade, forget to remember to water down the bandana for a cooling rinse, shoot a gu and a few pretzels, and back in the other direction, down into the space of the world split in half. Since the drizzle continues, I keep on putting time in the bank, working evenly paced 35 minute intervals to the aid stations: one Succeed and one ibuprofen every hour, and now mostly pretzels to keep a workable fuel mixture in the engine. I wonder, does this matter, since Bernd Heinrich (*Racing the Antelope*) has set records on Ben and Jerry's ?

OK, now halfway in just under six hours: find the drop bag and dig for dry socks over a thin coat of vaseline, get a new shirt, tie the shoes loosely, walk out with savory chicken noodle soup, and offer to anyone who might listen, but mostly for myself, "See you in about six and a half hours."

It doesn't get any better than this – just to think of the scope of running six hours, with six more to go – "Keep the faith. Never give up." The friendly sky still drizzles encouragement. I'm struggling to make the 35 minute intervals, the next one (from 50k to 55k) goes closer to 40 minutes. Digging now, approaching vision quest ground, if it will have me, I try to make the third leg in as close to three hours as I can. The next 5k takes a miserable 40 minutes, again. The leaders go by me for the third time, in their final burst to the finish, faces flushed, eyes bulging. What's left for me?

Tim the Greek from New York is left for me. Tim passes me first at 25k and again coming back, with about a 20 minute lead, as I approach the 50k turnaround. I think, "Don't chase him; let him come to you." I first met Tim the Greek (self-described) running at Catalina. He was with the peripatetic Henri Girault. Tim's very congenial. He says, "I never train… I just go to these runs, and we'll see what happens." The sun has come out, and it's getting hotter. I admire Tim and wish I knew his story. I think he's outrunning himself now, that he flies his moth too close to the light bulb. Sure enough, as I catch Tim at about 78k, he's listing to the right in an uncomfortable walk. Ultrarunners never one-up, always encourage, so I offer, "Way to go, Tim. There's some good refreshment ahead at the turnaround."

Tim's condition reminds me that now in the fourth quarter, I really have to focus, because in every sense, there isn't much left. I make the turn for the final 25k, ten minutes on the far side of nine hours, but still think I have a shot at a twelve hour finish. Funny how you still fight time, even after your best times are behind you. But like fear, time is a more pragmatic motivator than, "I'll just run as hard as I can for the next 15 miles." That doesn't work. I use my watch like a meat thermometer.

I snail from 75 to 80k in 45 minutes, 10 minutes slower than the earlier 5k intervals. Forget the twelve hour scenario. Now what's realistic? Again, some quick math in the head (there have been ultras where I couldn't do this). Now, a 12:45 finish or better becomes my new goal. While I can think pretty clearly to run faster, the body mechanism just won't cooperate. I try a short walk to limber and stretch, resuming a better pace, but that lasts about ten minutes before I shorten up. I'm still running, but in slow motion. I long for the next aid station, hoping it will revive me. I try Mountain Dew and get a mountainous dry mouth. Nothing sweet appeals. I drink from my CamelBak without breathing to mask the taste. No nausea, just dry-mouth. Where's the Magic? Pretzels and water work a little. I've got nine miles to go, and I think, "Why am I torturing myself? I wish I weren't here. And I won't ever eat another stupid pretzel; I can hardly swallow them, I'm so dry."

Passing the second to last aid station, 10k to go – "Just a measly 10k, c'mon man, get going! One hour and thirty minutes will get you a 12:30." I think only of the next step, the next aid station, the one under the tall highway bridge, and cool water's renewal. There it is, way off yonder, straight down the rail bed, looking improbably close. I go, not looking at my watch, but only at the bridge getting glacially closer to me.

"What can I get for you?" she asks, when I approach. It's so funny. A fresh set of legs, perhaps? I fumble in the tupperware, knocking over one cup of water she had carefully poured earlier, clutch a few Pringles and two remaining cups of water, one of which I pour on my empty head.

It's five before the hour now, with 5k left to finish. "What've you got ? Nothing to save now! Make it work! Go, go, go!" I will not look at my watch anymore. I will finish and earn that buckle. I will finish running as I have the entire way, though I may never run another ultra after this one. It's approaching dark. I want to go faster, but I can't. Damn the right knee and damn the toe blister; there's worse pain in not being able to go any faster than this pathetic shuffle.

And so into the finish - finishing is anticlimactic - I just stop. There's a feeling, "Isn't there something left for me to do, isn't there a way I can improve on what I've just done? Is it over? Can I have it back?"

The soulless, digital event timer says 12:35, and I am gratified. On this day, I've given all I can to the Withlacoochee and taken from it a 100k personal best that will last a lifetime. The next day on the plane back to Boston, a stewardess passes me a small bag of pretzels. I open it and eat them without a thought. Gratifying taste, pretzels. Now, as I write this, it's been less than two days, and I can even walk down the stairs without having to hold onto the banister like I did in the airport. Memory is short, isn't it?

———

MIWOK 100K
May 4, 2002

After Withlacoochee, I decide to try Marin County's famous Miwok 100k trail run. In the hills across the Golden Gate Bridge and San Francisco, Miwok has 9500 feet of vertical and another 9500 feet of descending terrain. It's not for beginners or people who allow distractions.

To prepare emotionally for other long runs, I read stories of improbable physical and psychological challenges, with survival endings that give the wisdom of self-knowledge not otherwise accessible, except through that experience. This time, I chose to read *Best Short Stories of 1999*, edited by Amy Tan. Her selections reflect on the nature of love relationships, which probe deep, often unconscious needs, manifest superficially in sweet boy/girl feelings, but with dark underlying complications.

A common thread in these stories joins the fabric of two separate lives: two people desiring love, more inclined to take it than give it, resulting in an incomplete and troubled dynamic, where conflict becomes the unwanted outcome. Naturally selfish motives stand in the way of potential fulfillment, right down to the basic differences between male and female psyche.

Man the performer, the wanderer, the battler, possessed with sexual hunger, faces woman, the nester, the incubator, the peacemaker; they need elements of each other, but they do not identify with the other's primal urgings. She wants her lover to settle, to listen, to care the way she cares, while he tends to view the relationship as a continuum of seduction contests. She thinks,"If you are nice to me I will be intimate," while he thinks, "If you are intimate with me I will be nice." Over time, they take each other's companionship for granted, not knowing that this relationship with one-sided premises is destined to fail. Selfish thinking dwells on what a relationship lacks, more than what it needs. This yields to misunderstanding, alienation, and loneliness. People want to be out of the trap they have put themselves in, projecting their selfishness into blame on their mate. It's easy to forget that if you do not give freely and unconditionally, you can expect little in return.

Traversing outbound from Pan Toll to Bolinas
and the turnaround at Olema

Photo by Don Lundell

I carry these thoughts with me from the foggy pre-dawn beach start, through fields high above the Pacific, and through the woods, ruminating on my relationship with Deedie: "Am I like the men in the book? Am I literally running away from what she needs and from what I need to give her? When she said goodbye to me, looking hurt, was she being selfish, or am I the one that's being selfish?"

By chance I meet Bob Boeder (*Hardrock Fever*), and we run and talk, until he pulls ahead before the 50 mile Pan Toll aid station. This pleasant interlude takes me away from those disquieting thoughts, but they return when I'm alone again. I've read Miwok reports on how the final 12 miles can be chilly when dark. I'm behind my planned pace, and know it will get chilly and dark. I'm prepared for neither, nor am I of a mind to run any longer. I quit right there at mile 50 and hitch a ride back to the finish.

"So what happened to you? Are you injured?" asks the kindly driver. "No. Woman problems," I answer.

I fly home, feeling down.

I understand that valued companionship can't be taken for granted, that it has to be nurtured. Maybe I've gone too far away, pursuing false self-affirmation, when I should recognize what I've been looking for is not "out there" but directly in front of me. I can't run ultras without first somehow neutralizing my wife's resentment toward them. I must work on this. I must give her more of my time, show her more consistently how much I care. I cannot always put myself first. She is so very important to me.

———

Having failed to complete Miwok, I don't see myself as a failure. To the contrary, I've learned something: long distance running allows me to shed little protective devices I've formed out of selfish convenience – the half-truths, the transparent pufferies, the projections of idealized, illegitimate self. These mind buffers that shaped an isolated self concept now are starting to melt away. I see my true self emerging out of the runner, dropping illusions along the way, more capable of facing life honestly. There's no hiding in ultrarunning, and you take more of your real self with you when the run is finished. I won't hide from the truth of our relationship, either. For my part, I must remove those sweepings out from under our rug; for my part, I must come clean.

It's more than just running; it's a purification rite, a cathartic process. In the days following, I feel unburdened, clearer thinking, more able to give myself to her. Yes, I will go back, to start up one more evolution of training for the next ultra. But first there's much needed home-work to be done.

DAY AT THE BEACH

It's the third straight day of 90+ degree heat and high humidity, and not a breath of wind. I go into the dog pen and lift the canoe out through the gate, setting it in the driveway. I hose the dirt off and hoist it onto the car rack. Deedie packs a lunch with cold drinks in the cooler.

It's so hot you can't think without effort. We're gliding north on route 128, and I bring an old tease, wondering how far we'll get before the canoe gets swept off the roof, cart-wheeling along the pavement. It stays securely tied all the way to Annisquam. Seeing the ocean, we're already cooler.

Deedie carries the picnic, paddles and beach chairs while I shoulder the canoe down the path by the tennis court, across the plank way to the beach. We load up first, then go for a swim. The surface water is warm, while nearer the bottom where crabs scuttle, it's cold. I flutter kick down into the coolest layer until I can't hold my breath any longer. We launch.

Across the channel we see dense crowds at Wingaersheek Beach. We dismiss the idea of landing there, instead striking west toward the less populous Essex side. The canoe cuts through calm ocean over a sandbar, and we look at dark shapes in deepening waters, imagining weeds, rocks, rays, even scary monsters. Our own reflections mirror-mug at us.

One last hard stroke carries us to a soft beach landing. With the tide receding, we keep the canoe partly in the water, using it for a picnic table, our beach chairs on either side. Cold fruity drinks, pasta salad, carrots, pretzels, cheese, strawberries, a plum; we savor them and the scene before us: ocean, bathers, boats. It's peaceful and we cheer ourselves. Deedie's amused by my straw hat, saying I look like the animal tamer in the story, "Curious George," that we've read countless times to our children. We swim again.

Back in the canoe, we explore the inlets and beaches across the channel on the Annisquam side. Large, fumy boats push waves at us as we cautiously thread a safe course through the threatening chop. We stroke into a tiny bay, lined with bathers standing knee and waist deep, hands on hips, talking and watching.

Three greenheads (deer flies) lie bludgeoned at my sunburned feet on the bottom of the boat. Paddling in the tippy chop, it's risky to stop and scratch the middle of your back – is it a bite bug or a salt itch? But when the little blue-eyed bastards whirl around to land on the knee, whack! Then whack again, and finally, whack !!!

Scissor-kicking down to the coldest water and the scuttling crabs, we turn to view the sleek green bottom of the canoe, and its security. The sweat is gone, but the burn stays on our shoulders and thighs: time to layer on loose clothes, Bedouin style. We sight a summer cottage through the bush cover on the point. Young people congregate on the deck. We were young; we remember them. We pass a man red as a lobster, unaware of it, rigging his sailboat to go out. What will he look like when he returns?

Stroking with the tide we pass the lighthouse, discussing the houses that go by: "Do you like the deck on that one, would we like to live in that one, which one is our favorite?" Deedie suggests we swim in the next cove. I see we're close to the takeout beach, but ask myself, "Why not? What's the rush?" Her idea, it's the best swim of the day. We float.

It's so hot - the canoe thwart presses into my burned shoulders and neck, one labored step up, then another, through the bushes on the path, to the lawn where the car waits with its key hidden atop the front tire.

On the way home, Deedie tells me she likes going to Annisquam. So do I. Forty-five years ago when I was ten, my family came here for a week , from land-bound Milwaukee. I learned how to dig for steamer clams and capture crabs to put in the small leaky punt we boys used to explore. Again, thirty years ago on a cold November afternoon, I built a fire here on the beach for steamers, a brief refuge from the mind's pressure cooker of business school. And countless other visits. We go back, we find the people we were.

———

HALLIBURTON FOREST 50 MILER
September 7, 2002

Halliburton Forest is a 50,000-acre expanse about 170 miles north and east of Toronto. There are three events: a 100 miler, a 50 miler, and a 50k, all on the same trails and starting simultaneously at 6 a.m. Race director Helen Malmberg organizes things perfectly: the well-stocked aid stations, the pre and post race dinners, great volunteers, and the companionship of runners, all create a special weekend in a special place.

I make Halliburton a regrouping event, four months after my drop at Miwok. This is a back-to-basics crusade for me – train properly, execute intelligently. The added dimension of camping there appeals to me, as I hope this might elevate my spirit and improve my focus.

Looking out from the tent on Macdonald Lake after the runners' dinner Friday night, I feel the setting absorb me; I am now another feature in the forest, like the trails I will follow the next day. I sleep well in quiet darkness. Waking before 4 a.m., I start a fire for warmth and coffee. Holding the hot drink in both hands, I look up through the dark to see a sky filled with stars – millions of them. It's still and completely quiet. I feel I belong right here in this dawn. I imagine what I will do in the next few minutes and throughout the day: I will run purposefully and I will carry the forest's urging.

The course is 25 miles out and back, producing the 50. 100 mile runners make it a double out and back. Aid stations are spaced approximately in 5 mile intervals. Though it is still dark at the start, most of the 110 runners don't use flashlights, as the first five miles are on gravel road. Just pick your feet up and run a little flat-footed and slower, to avoid twisting an ankle on a rock. It's going to be a long day, and runners start out slow to warm up – nobody's in a hurry yet.

RD Helen Malmberg is also an accomplished ultrarunner – I ran behind Helen for many miles at the Slough of Despond 50k.

I have a CamelBak with about 40 oz. Accelerade mix, gu, and lots of Succeed electrolyte tabs and ibuprofen. Aid stations have E-load, a buffered electrolyte mix, and various standard food items like pretzels, nuts, chips, fruit, trail mix, etc. I plan to sip from my CamelBak between aid station drinks and to eat something at every stop. After an hour and a half, I begin taking one electrolyte tab and one ibuprofen at hourly intervals.

Forest roads and trails alternate regularly. Going out, I mark transition points on my watch so that I'll have a better idea of pace coming back. I figure 10 hours would have been doable in cooler temps, but 10 ½ hrs is now more reasonable, given the rising heat. After the 1st aid station at five miles, we join the Krista Trail, rising up, then down, covering about two and a half miles At a five mile per hour pace, I'm comfortably moving along in the cool morning without too much effort, conscious that this is slightly ahead of my overall pace estimate. Who knows the perfect trade off between going out slowly to work into a rhythm or upping the tempo early because it's the coolest part of the day? I know that starting out too fast will burn energy stores needed later, and can significantly increase the risk of crashing. I accept this risk; I'm eager.

Road and single track trail alternate to the 10 mile aid station at Black Lake - my elapsed time is two hours: a steady, even pace. Terrain on the Red and the King and James Trails is rocky and requires more concentration. Coming through dense bush, I get hit on the top of the head by a monster bee, whose venomous sting brings a throbbing pain that distracts me for about twenty minutes until the poison diffuses.

I come into the 15.6 mile aid station at three hours and twelve minutes: " OK, now I'm getting behind the ten hour pace, but that's no surprise. Let's see: I can make the 20 mile aid station in less than an hour; after all, it's only 4.4 miles." But I'm slower than that, as this stretch includes four miles on the uneven Osprey Trail as well as on hot, sun-exposed road. I struggle to make the next stop in about one hour and five minutes. This puts a ten and a half hour finish into question.

Gord England catches up with me, and we run together for about thirty-five minutes, chatting about the Ontario Ultra Series events, and the Halliburton course. He says many of the Canadians here are getting psyched for the Sri Chinmoy 24 hour event next weekend. I think, "Wow, a lot of these folks are pretty hardcore." Time passes quickly, and soon the 25 mile turnaround is in sight. My time is 5 hours, 7 minutes.

Monica Scholz's Dad runs the turnaround aid station at mile 25, all day and all night. Monica is recognized as Canada's most accomplished female ultrarunner.

In my drop bag I have a change of socks, vaseline for the feet, food and drink. I'm determined to transition through the aid stations faster than in previous runs, so I judge my feet are OK and don't need a change of socks. The aid station is grand – big awning over the table and a grill for more substantial food to offer 100 milers at the 75 mile point. But I can't dawdle. I whip out of there, figuring there's still a shot at ten and a half hours. Going back, I can work the splits, now that I have familiarity with the course.

I slow to a crawl after the 30 mile aid station, going over the rocky, hilly sections, to protect myself from the trip and fall that takes away so much energy. This would be the first long trail run I've done without falling or banging up my toes. I've learned that fatigue combined with anxiety to maintain a predetermined pace can lead to unnecessary mistakes; better to slow down, relax, and work smoothly.

After a long slog to the 35 mile aid station, now at 7 hours 20 minutes, I'm thinking 10 1/2 hours will be a stretch. Brian Magee looks to be struggling as he tells me he's taken a fall on his hip and is hurting. "I figured I'd just make it to the next aid station, then evaluate, but I'm still going," he says. We run along together, sharing stories, and I realize "time" is not as important as enjoying the day and finishing strong: more walking now.

At the 40 mile aid station I load up with ice and water. Here comes Victor Hickey, 100 miler, through his mile 60, looking good. I marvel that he's going nearly twice as fast and twice as long as I am. I can wonder about the others, but what they do doesn't help me; I have only myself to deal with. I know I'm going to finish, but it will be slower than I wanted. I think this is not so disappointing, just what the day has in store for me – I'm going along as well as I can. Now at 8 hours 40 minutes, I think maybe 11 hours could be doable. The good news: I have no physical problems, so on we go.

This is my eighth run of 50 miles or more. In the first few, I would psyche up for an epic struggle, using all kinds of mental tricks to put me through the finish. Now, I'm working Halliburton as nothing more than a calculated and determined effort of focus and execution. I've read so many times in ultra reports: "just have fun," but not until Haliburton did I actually arrive there. The closest I've gotten was to think that the fun part comes when it's over. This time, because I can embrace the moment, the majesty of the surroundings, and the bonding company of so many soul mates running with me, I truly enjoy the final miles.

Back onto the Krista trail and I know at the end of it there's a road and just 5 miles of easy running left. Going out, a 100 miler told me this trail was tougher coming back, and I remember that, as it tracks up and up, forcing me to walk. Earlier in the day, we were skipping down this part in the cool morning; it's so different now. I hear Brian coming up behind, and we resume chatting with no hint of competition as we walk and run when we can. I usually don't enjoy talking much, but Brian and I are on the same wavelength.

I feel mild cramping in the middle of my back, but when I put my hands on the back of my hips and press with my thumbs, it tends to subside. My physical self wants to stop, but stopping is not an option. I've trained too hard and too well to allow that to happen. Halliburton is a must, to put that Miwok DNF behind me.

Plus, I'm in the company of great athletes, and I want to show my stuff. There's Patricia Sommers, running the 50 miler. After a scary bear encounter in the dark at mile 70 in the 100 miler two years ago (she finished), she returned in 2001 to set a course record in the 50. There's Rolly Portelance, who I will witness finishing his sixtieth 100 mile run tomorrow morning. There's Monica, who ran 23 100 milers last year – we greet her as we near the 50 mile finish, and she heads back out for 50 more, to run through the night. Then comes Kevin Sayers, whose ultrarunning website is the best resource available for good advice on how to prepare for an ultra, and the literate and spiritual John Prohira, who brought several first timers with him from Rochester. These "gods" inspire me to think beyond my discomfort, to continue on without complaint.

Brian and I stay together through the finish, feeding on each other, running a little, and walking the hills. With a half mile to go, I want to run this last bit, but slow to walk when Brian does, for the slightest incline. We cross under the banner at 11:13. Spontaneously, we shake hands and say "Thanks" in the same breath.

At the Friday dinner, Helen asked everyone to stand up individually and say who they were and what event they intended to run. That gave us a warm sense of community and familiarity, and I think it helped me run better. It's a loner sport, but I felt grand in the company of others of the same mind.

I enjoy another good sleep in my tent, just off the trail, one mile from the finish. Waking at four Sunday morning, I hear a couple 100 milers go by in the dark and imagine their joy as they head into the finish. As I look out one last time over the glassy lake, a red sun rises through the trees, and a single loon pops up out of nowhere, going about its hunt. Nature's dispassionate rhythm thrums continuously here, while people only visit when convenient.

Before I leave Halliburton Forest Sunday morning,
I stop at the finish in the rising dawn and stand by
the warming fire that Helen has lit. One by one,
sometimes together, sometimes nearly an hour apart,
the 100 mile finishers come into view down the road,
approaching completion. I watch them. I study their
exhaustion and their joy. I take these moments away
with me and hold them close, in the hope that one
day, I might be as fortunate as they are.

———

PORTLAND MAINE MARATHON
October 7, 2002

My idea of a successful event includes good planning
as well as good execution. After the roadwork and
beginning the taper, you get a sense of relative fitness
and can gauge a finishing time from that. You can
check the weather forecast to see if conditions will in
any way impair that target, such as high temperatures
or heavy percipitation. The Portland forecast calls for
temperatures in the fifties and lower sixties, with a
light breeze. The course is described as relatively flat.
As the day nears, I figure there is nothing to keep me
from pushing myself to the edge if it feels right. I
think before I leave for Portland that four hours and
ten minutes is the number.

You can have good days and not so good days, and there's no telling why. Even after a good taper, the right food, and plenty of rest beforehand, when you get underway you have to feel yourself out to see what kind of a day it's going to be.

I leave the house at five a.m. for the hour and three-quarter ride to Portland. The sun comes up just as I cross into New Hampshire. Already I'm getting juiced at the idea of covering great distances in a day's time: drive Boston to Portland, run twenty-six miles, then back home before three in the afternoon. Cool. Now for that matter of the 26.2 miles.

Smaller marathons suit me better because there are fewer distractions. I find it easier to relax, easier to focus on mechanics, efficiency and nourishment. To facilitate a smooth ride, I try to get mentally detached from my physical self; this makes it easier to figure out what's going on during the run and how to best deal with circumstances that require problem solving.

So we start, and my first mile is an 8:45 pace. This is too fast - I'm relaxed and not pushing it, but I know I'll have to back down a little bit later. A 9 minute per mile pace gets a 3:56 finish, while a 10 minute pace gets 4:22. My objective beforehand was a 9:30 pace, but early in the run, I think, "Let's see how long I can maintain a 9 minute pace." Advancing the objective early is a very typical rookie mistake that nearly always results in a crash reducing walk and a broken spirit before the finish. I'm aware of this as I go along, but I accept my decision.

I know from my ultra experience that if I bonk I can still shuffle along at 12 minutes per mile. Should this happen at mile 20, say, I'll still finish close to 4:10.

Around mile 6, I'm twenty-five seconds ahead of the 9 minute per mile pace. At 10 miles I've given more time back and rate closer to even 9's. "Relax and flow," I say. "Use your arms and extend your stride comfortably." At the halfway point I'm at two hours and know if I can match this for the next 13.1 miles, I might break four hours.

The contest evolves. I'm riding the edge, feeling good about the challenge. Now it's more of a struggle, but I'm not yet pushing at the 90% level. Through 20 miles with 6.2 to go, I see I have one hour and five minutes to break four hours. In my training runs I've consistently managed just this in the second half of a 13 mile run, but now there are 20 miles behind me instead of 6.5. "Right," I say, "but these are the terms of event running; you've trained and rested, and extra demands can possibly be met."

Conditions remain favorable – it's still not hot, I'm hydrated and pushing down gu. My stride has shortened a bit, so I concentrate on arm swing, hip swivel, leg extension, and deep belly breathing. I think, "When I get a little further into this, I can put the hammer down through the last few miles, above the 90% effort level."

Three miles left, and I've got twenty-five minutes to make four hours. I can do it if I reach deeper and hold up physically. The detachment now has mind imploring body, "Go!" And body responding, "I'm going the best I can!" My leg turnover flags even more; I'm not close to bonking, but reserves are fast being used up. With 2 miles left, I tell myself if I can pull off 8 minute miles for just 2 miles - I still have a shot!

My body cannot produce 8 minute miles, however. I feel like I'm running in sand. This hasn't yet degenerated into 12 minute miles, so I'm satisfied with my progress. I know four hours will pass, and I'll be short of the finish - now just striding, breathing heavily, deeply, riding the edge. I see the digital clock above the finish line reading four hours, two minutes and change.

Then I'm through at four and three. The four hour barrier remains out of reach, but I've beaten my four and ten estimate, and I'm not trashed. My on-the-fly objective kept me pushing, motivated and challenged. This is what we do when we run long: evaluate the training experience, set the objective, take the test, see your result, and think, "That wasn't too bad," or "I can do better next time." Accept what you have done and learn from it.

Driving home, I wonder, "Maybe a little more speed work, and some weights in the next training cycle, and I can push the envelope out a little further."

––––

ROCKY RACCOON 50 MILER
February 1, 2003

I went to Huntsville, Texas for two reasons. It was Mickey Rollins' last year as race director, and I wanted to meet him after reading about him on the internet. Too, RR is firstly remembered as a 100 mile event (this was the second year that a 50 miler was included), and I longed to observe the century runners, as I hold them in reverential awe. At 72, the oldest century runner said Friday night at the briefing and feed, "I ran a 'hundred' ten months ago, and it was so hard I told myself I'd never try it again… but I forgot." In the lodge before the 100 started on Saturday morning, someone remarked to us 50 milers without a hint of condescension, "So you're the folks who are going on the fun run?"

This is like the Stone Cat Ale 50: four 12 ½ mile loops. It's less hilly than Mt. Hood, Catalina, Bull Run, and Halliburton. There are roots to contend with, but also stretches where you can run freely (almost half of it).

———

We start at 6:30, half an hour after the 100 milers, and use flashlights for the first few miles. With first light, we're on a runnable jeep road, going out to a turnaround at the first aid station (3.4 miles). I ask how far to the following aid station and hear, "Three point-seven miles." This is accurate for those running the 100, but not for us. After returning down the jeep road, then cutting back into the woods, I figure about 20 minutes more to the next stop for food and drink. Twenty minutes pass, then 30: still no aid station. As I wonder where it is, or if I might be lost, a root sends me crashing to a hard face plant (the least distraction will make you pay). Then I remember that Joe Prusaitis (Mickey's successor RD) told me there was nearly a six mile stretch between aid stations at one point for the 50 milers. This must be that section. A little squirrely right left, right left, then down to a boardwalk crossing at the end of the lake. Serge Arbona, the lead 100 miler passes me, and in a bit I pass another 50 miler who asks, "How far do you think it is to the next aid station?" I think about four minutes, and sure enough, there it is four minutes later. It helps to have your bearings for pacing purposes; now I feel more secure about the layout.

The aid station volunteer says about 3.7 miles to the start/finish turnaround, which seems a little long to me, as I'm on a 2:20 loop pace objective and by that measure should have about a half hour left to go. Coming back to the park access road, I mark the time from there to the turnaround and find it's about 13 minutes. I complete the first lap exactly at 2:20, feeling very good about my pacing work to this point.

From my drop bag I put a bottle of Clip mix into my CamelBak, grab a few pb&j quarters and potatoes, and head out for lap number two. From my Stone Cat

Rocky Raccoon runners circle Lake Raven, in
Huntsville, Texas State Park

time and from what I'd read about RR's terrain
I figure 10 to 10 ½ hours total will be a realistic
objective. I keep a steady pace through the
second lap and find from the squirrely part it's
45 minutes to the finish. I've had time to plan a
faster transition there: drop bags were in front of
the turnaround cone and the aid station table.
On the first loop Mickey cautioned, "Be sure to
go around the cone," which I did before going to
the drop bag. But then I had to double back to
the table, losing precious seconds. So the second
time through I go straight for the drop bag (and
another bottle of Clip), bringing out a "tssk" of
disapproval from Mickey, sitting comfortably
there in a folding chair. "You have to go around
the cone." I reply, "NO – I've just spent 2 ½ hours
figuring out a faster transition, and I'm going to
the drop bag first." This causes much hilarity with
Mickey and others who seem astonished that I'd
question the RD's command. Chuckles on that

one, as I go around the cone for
lap three.

It's warmer now, and the heat starts getting to
me (I've been training in 15 degree temps back
East). In the early morning it was 41 degrees, but
now it's closer to 70, and no breeze. I'm taking
one Succeed tab and one ibuprofen hourly. Even
a minor grade jeep trail up to the next aid station
drags me to a walk. There I linger a minute to eat
and drink, hoping to energize. When I mark time
at the spillway, I see my lap pace has slowed by 15
minutes from that of the first two laps. Now the 10
hour objective looks like a stretch.

Here comes a string of 100 milers; each one
working out his/her plan, some walking, some
paired up in a purposeful trot. I'm thrilled to see
Ann Trason, one of our legends. There goes Rolly
Portelance (his 63rd 100) with no shirt and a
single water bottle. One guy about 6'3" has the
strangest shuffle, but he glides past me – it works
for him. I wonder on them all.

I finish the third lap with 7 ½ hours elapsed - a
2:45 lap. I consider, then dismiss the possibility of
trying to run the 4th loop in 2 ½ hours to make 10
hours. "Whatever," I think, "just keep going." From
the start/finish to the next aid station I pass into
the low point that seems to come nearly every
time in the 35-40 mile range. Doubt creeps in to
question my resolve: "Why are you doing this? This
is so hard; maybe this isn't what you should be
doing, maybe this will be your last one." Taunted

by these doubts, I still hold on, pressing to the finish. I ask an aid station volunteer for some "distance aid"; he says there are only 9 more miles to go.

I begin to forget the difficulty I'm in, thinking, "Jeez, I've run 9 miles hundreds of times - it's not that much." It's the smell the barn syndrome. I go for the kill. I recall Red Spicer's immortal words, "I hammered down the trail, passing rocks and trees like they were standing still." Reality blurs. I'm in that red zone where fatigue doesn't matter and the goal is within reach. There's no reason to hold back. I can't remember the last time I took the pills, so I just take them again. Looking at my watch as I come to the squirrely part, I see just over 45 minutes to make 10 1/2 hours – my new goal.

The hunt intensifies. I reach my hardest speed, not risking a fall. The scene blurs still more. Once more crossing the boardwalk, I scan for just one slumbering alligator to remember (they're in there, but hidden): nothing. Then left through the mud hole instead of right on the dry edge, as I'd learned in prior laps – details like this are hard to remember after ten hours of running.

Arriving at the last aid station I hurriedly pour a little water for the last stretch. This will take half an hour if I can go as fast as the first two laps, and I have 33 minutes to break 10 1/2 hours. I force a run up the inclines where I had walked in the third lap. Reaching the park access road, I see about

13 minutes to break the 10 1/2 mark. You've been there, I bet, and it's great, the point where you're going full out and it's wildly hard but the idea of the finish dominates all thought and feeling. You want it bad, and you don't care about anything else. In my mind I'm flying. The seven year old girl I pass, walking with her parents probably wonders "Why is that man's face so red, when he's hardly running?"

Then the last stretch to the finish, and I have two minutes, or is it three, or one? I can't think, I just bust it down the final 300 yards – let the clock be the judge. People cheer encouragement as I cross under the banner, the wash of accomplishment overwhelming feelings of fatigue. I've bagged another 50 miler, this one in 10:29:33 and middle of the pack – a good showing for me.

Returning to the motel, I find dinner, have a good sleep, get up for breakfast and go back to the site before dawn to see the 100 milers finish. I observe, drinking it in. Soon it's time to head for the airport. As I drive out the access road, my car lights lead me away from the evocative scenes I've witnessed in the dark, such as the celebration by two runners of their "one sunrise 100." By the time I'm in the Houston airport, it seems such an odd, artificial place in contrast to Huntsville Park. I imagine a sign reading: "Welcome back to the unreal world."

Like the aged runner, I also forgot: I started Rocky Raccoon anticipating the satisfaction of finishing, while forgetting I would first have to pass through that hard low point leading to the other side, full of clarity and uninhibited energy. Now I remember why we willingly draw ourselves through that stretch of pain and doubt: to prove that we can endure, to emerge from the deep with the prize.

Rocky Raccoon is a good one, even if you only go 50 miles.

———

CHAPTER FOUR – HIGH GROUND

On that Rocky Raccoon Saturday in February, 2003, the space shuttle Columbia disintegrated in the sky overhead. None of us knew it, but as we ran in contained self-absorption, seven astronauts and pieces of their ship scattered down in a wide swath just miles north and east of us. Flying back to Boston, I thought how short and frail and precious this life is, despite all the protective constructs that allow us to pretend otherwise. When challenged, they are like sand castles built at low tide.

Before I die, I want to share my love more completely with Deedie. I want to run 100 miles, too. Do these conflict ? My ambition is further complicated when Deedie tells me she's worried that if I try, I might badly hurt myself. What I hear is a voice coming from the sand castle. She wants me for herself, but I want me for myself more. If there's risk in running 100 miles, I'll accept it for the Magical rewards that may come to me in finishing. I must discover myself before I die.

———

MIWOK 100K
May 3, 2003

Three days before Miwok, I contemplate unfinished business from last year. In this training cycle, I've worked harder than ever; weight lifting, ab work, three 29 mile runs, one back to back set of 20's, and four consecutive weeks of 55, 60, 53, and 60 miles. It's been easier, compared to training for Rocky Raccoon, when New England was cold and the weather was at times a shut down factor.

Studying my ultra finishing times and those at Miwok, I calculate my objective at 15 ½ hours. Training has gone well. I've clocked a recent low for my standard 10 mile run at 1 hour 26 minutes and ran one hour 56 minutes for 13 miles in my last up tempo run. I've switched to a lighter weight running shoe from the brand I've used for years. I've switched to Hammer Gel (the flask containers are easier to manage) from those one ounce rip-and-tear gu packets, and I will try Succeed Amino after Clip and Accelerade, progressively through the 62 mile Miwok distance. Weather is expected to be rainy, but cooler; this may help. I'm set on being more patient this time, and I'm as ready as I can be.

As usual I've found interesting reading to help me prepare mentally. Why do some 100 mile runners say upon finishing, "I'll never do this again," only to return? Why do furloughed soldiers after enduring the horrors of war find a curious longing to return to battle? It's the face of opposites. Visiting the edge, we find the center. Reaching exhaustion, we find how to relax. Daily trivia and life's cheap thrills leave us longing for a real deal. Going deep, we hold on to something worth remembering. Answers to such questions are found in *Running Through the Wall* –

Personal Encounters With the Ultramarathon, edited by Neal Jamison and in *A Step Beyond: A Definitive Guide to Ultrarunning*, edited by Don Allison. As we stand in dark drizzle, RD "Tropical John" Medinger tells us to reflect on how fortunate we are to be here, capable of doing this, to enjoy the scenery of the day, and, as he advised last year, to have fun.

You have to learn how to relax. You cannot compare your progress to the progress of others, because they are not you. Time is your friend; it is not something to beat. It will take time. Body is athlete, mind is coach. You will feed yourself, take fluids and electrolytes, even ibuprofen. Your feet get the attention of a teen face, because they make abrasive contact hour upon hour, and must not be allowed to become a reason to stop. You will tell yourself that there are reasons to stop, but nearly all of them are just pleadings of a weak soul. You will endure if you stay ahead of your problems. Anticipate, don't presume.

After John signals the start with a simple "Go," I let the faster and more eager ones go ahead, crossing the beach with high flat steps to keep the sand out of my shoes. And soon up on the road, we're climbing 800 feet over three miles, with a rewarding view of Golden Gate Bridge - south posts in the dawning sun, north posts shrouded in fog. I see Terry and John Rhodes (movie stars from A Race For The Soul, a fine documentary on the Western States 100), and I know their pace will be measured, as mine should be. I contain my enthusiasm to run faster and follow them for a few miles.

At the Bunker Road (5.5 miles) aid station, there's "Tropical John," assisting at the water stop with an open mouth half gallon pitcher. I ask if I can drink straight out of it: "What, you don't even have a water bottle?" he asks, letting me drink. Many runners carry 24 ounce water bottles in their hands, while I use the CamelBak. In it are two scoops of Accelerade with 40 ounces of water, enough to last to the Pan Toll (mile 21) aid station, if I drink additional water at the aid stations along the way. There, I have left two full bottles, one with Clip and one with Amino, for 20-35 miles and 50-62 miles respectively, plus Clip and Amino powder in a bottle to carry and fill at mile 35, to last until mile 50. At Pan Toll I have two pairs of shoes, socks, shirts, a windbreaker, vaseline, band aids, Hammer Gel flasks, and two turkey sandwiches. I've planned meticulously. In my pockets I carry Succeed electrolytes and ibuprofen, Tums, Jolt caffeinated gum, and two vitamin tablets.

The climbs to Tennessee Valley (11.2 miles) and Muir Beach (15.3 miles) aid stations are muddy from the falling rain, and my shoes hold on to a heavy layer of clay as I plod along. The descent to Muir Beach is very slick and watery; I brake to guard against falling backward with a slip-out foot plant. So far, so good; I haven't done anything stupid yet. To my right there's a small group of runners disappearing into the fog, having made a wrong turn. We shout at them, "This way!"

In the valley sections from Muir Beach to the big climb (1385 feet from miles 16-19) and then later out from miles 53-58, gnarly poison oak reaches out into the narrow path, trying to give me a little present to remember the day. Auto-correcting from slips in the mud, I gyrate to dodge these little tendrils. Rubber band man!

I accept the slow climb to Pan Toll, rehearse my aid station routine, and take in the scene: yes, this is a splendid day! The sun has come out intermittently, warming open areas between clusters of pine and eucalyptus. Look, here's a photographer. I tell myself I will buy a picture from him only if I finish.

With new socks, shoes and shirt, fuel and encouragement from onlookers at Pan Toll I head down the ridge to Bolinas (mile 27.7) with glorious views of the coastline and bold blue blooms of flowers contrasting with the dominant deep green grass. Occasional rivulets stream down the slope we're traversing, offering the chance to dip a hat or handkerchief for a rinse. I gladly accept what the day offers.

From Bolinas to the turnaround at Olema (35.4 miles) the rains have left unavoidable pond crossings in the jeep road. After skirting the edges, cat-like, I begin following the example of returning runners, who simply splash straight through them, dry feet long gone. Then finally out into a clearing, and with about two miles until the turnaround, the distance stretches. I remind myself, "Be patient, let it come to you – don't force it. Flow down there, instead of trying to reel it in." I make Olema 27 minutes in front of the

Miwok's climb to Pan Toll offers spectacular
views of the Pacific Ocean.

Photo by Don Lundell

cut off, with time to wring the mud out of my socks
and refuel (takes seven minutes). Aid station strategy
should balance getting in and out quickly, while still
taking care of needs that if not attended to could
hasten a bonk, an injury, or the dread DNF.

Now back. There's always a charge of energy when
you know you're directed toward the finish (even if
it's a marathon away). Long walk up the slope and
out of the clearing into the watery woods where the
real work begins. This section seems to go on and on,
I think because it's shady and mostly uphill. As I grind
glacially towards aid at Bolinas (mile 43.2), I spend
miles thinking, "When I get there, I'll rinse the mud
out of my socks and shoes – then how fine my feet
will feel." Here's a spectator, encouraging the runner

ahead of me with "You're looking good, just a mile to the aid station." Then to me, "Boy, you look real tired." But I'm not real tired: I take his comment as a very unnecessary negative thought and quickly dismiss it. Approaching aid, I wriggle my muddy toes inside the shoes and, feeling no pain, elect not to stop. Save time. Show that "real tired" dude something. Then out of the woods into the fields again, climbing irregularly to Pan Toll (mile 50). This is a tough stretch with side hill traverses, and the idea is not to dwell on circumstances, just keep moving as well as possible. Walk, shuffle, walk, run a bit. At Pan Toll I go with a full change of shirt, shoes and socks, washing the feet and pin pricking a toe blister, then a band aid and thin layer of vaseline.

This takes more than fifteen minutes, and I go out having dropped my pills, returning to retrieve them after a moving inventory check reveals they're missing. Maybe three minutes lost there. There's time gained and time lost. Sometimes it seems I'm slower than time, and sometimes it's slower than me. Some time today, I'll finish. I remember not to dwell on time – that's stressful – but rather fix on the path, the placement of footsteps, the chances to really run, not forcing those either when I should walk (any upslope). Flow, flow and go.

While trying to swallow the potato chips I've chewed and pissing discreetly along the side of the trail, I start to dry heave. There's no uptake because my stomach's nearly empty, but I keep heaving. I sip from the CamelBak tube and chew a Tums to calm down.

The downhill after mile 50 marks a big psychological turning point. I know I will finish from here, in three hours and change; just monitor the system: electrolytes, fluids, Hammer Gel, ibuprofen, and bites of food at the two remaining aid stations. Everything's working, and I'm reasonably comfortable. I chew a couple of pieces of caffeinated gum. Working up the extremely steep gradients before aid at Highway 1 (55 miles) and after Tennessee Valley (mile 58.4) I think, "This is cruel and unusual" to myself, but hold the spoken words because they're negative; I need positives here. Soldier up one step at a time, get on with it. By now the downhills hurt my toes as they compress against the toe box; it's too steep to stride, making the steep ups easier than the steep downs.

Stan Jensen's chicken noodle soup at Tennessee Valley was promised me by a volunteer at Pan Toll. I see a tall jackrabbit dart through the brush, then flush a covey of game birds up into the heavy air. My thoughts return to the soup. As I reach the aid station, Stan approaches me with, "What can I get you?" Oh, savory moment. "Chicken noodle soup," I say. He: "We have lentil." Me: "Lentil?" He: "Yes, lentil soup. It's good." I sip a little. It's not chicken noodle. It's what the day offers. "Thank you for the soup, Stan," and I go on.

As light fades into darkness, I put on my green LED flashlight. Its beam presents comforting companionship. It will be my escort in the few short miles to the finish. Glow sticks mark turns at intersections. Now there's pavement – a very pleasant surprise, as I can stride without worrying about mud, rocks, and toe bangers. There's an intersection with no glow stick. In the dark I follow the pavement past a fence, partway across to the edge of a cliff, and stop abruptly there. How would this day change if I'd just kept going out into space, where gravity and rocks below would take over? Scary thought – I one-eighty out of there to the intended trail, and soon see the lights of Rodeo Beach far below. It cannot be too long now. Again, the idea is not to dwell on time but on the steps leading down, not to worry when the path seems to turn away from the lights, to remind myself the finish will come to me if I let time pass.

Now it's all right here in front of me ("Nice downhill finish," says the website); the fences, the lights everywhere, the volunteers, and the final turn into the canopy shelter with the big digital clock speeding to 15:32:59, where time stops for me with a race volunteer's pencil entry. I sit on an ice chest under the barbecue tent. I'm not hungry; I'm full in a different way. It's 12:15 a.m. in Boston – time to let go of time and head for bed.

———

JUST DO IT

When our children were little, we would go to a pool that had a high dive. They wanted to try it but were naturally afraid. We'd watch people climb the ladder, creep out to the end of the diving board, and stare down. Unable to overcome their fear, they'd turn around and cautiously descend to more familiar spaces. I took the willing Chloe up with me and holding her securely in my arms, jumped. Then Lila. I will always remember the triumphant looks on their faces when they surfaced with me. So it was no surprise to us when, soon after, they went off the high dive by themselves.

When I went to outpatient therapy to work my way out of alcoholism, the psychiatrist asked me to tell her who I am. I started by describing my big-time job, then my family, my physical features, then past accomplishments. She tried again, "But, who are you, really?" I suspected some kind of trap. She clearly saw a person in conflict, who could only come to well-being by working to reconcile opposing components of self-recognition. My jigsaw puzzle was forcibly assembled, pieces stuck out of place, held together by my stubborn, willful, erroneous vision of self.

Slowly I came to think, never accept what you are, always strive to become the person you want to be. In this present world, people are regularly introduced to technology that seems nothing short of miraculous – things that change the way they live. No small wonder, then, that I should hope to experience sudden spiritual enlightenment, or satori, by running 100 miles. I've already tried booze and drugs, and they didn't do it.

Every summer we all go to Deedie's family summer home in Maine to enjoy friendships, clean air, the cold ocean and its islands, tennis and golf. Typically, Deedie and the children make an extended stay, while I book vacation time from work to join them off and on through the summer. In 2003, I sent in my Vermont 100 application, picturing a window of opportunity in which Deedie would be in Maine, and I would be in Boston, "working." For this to set up in the right way, I needed to eliminate the potential for her disquieting objections. The Vermont 100 would be my stealth meeting with destiny.

———

VERMONT 100 MILE RUN
July 19, 2003

In the wee morn, about 20 hours after the start, a companion runner says, "Just think, the winner is already on his third dream by now." Others pick up, mentioning the shower, the meal, the warm bed, and finishing in daylight on the same day. This is not for us; this is impossible for us, but we will finish as we can. Vermont's fifteenth running is my first 100 mile run.

In the range of ultrarunners, from those just starting out who hold much in awe to the veterans who think even a run write-up compromises the purity of their experience, I'm moving along that continuum. I can dream big, and I dare to fail. In the hills around

Woodstock on July 19th and 20th, I went into that dream and made it reality. Fulfilled and depleted, I want to share this with those also moving in this way, because experience helps. And for those who elect not to run ultras, remember that one person's view of extreme is another's of simple. Playing "Chopsticks" on the piano is as challenging to me as Glenn Gould's Bach sonatas were to him.

I ran the Miwok 100k in May as a training run, starting out slow and staying slow, finishing in 15 ½ hours (15 minute miles). There was some gas left in the tank. I figure if I can run the first 68 miles of Vermont at a 15.8 min per mile pace and the final 32 miles at a 17.8 min per mile pace, it will take 27.5 hours. So I set the over/under at 27 1/2 to 28 hours. You must have a game plan, and it must be rehearsed. You have to stay with it, never going faster than planned unless you're close enough to the finish to burn energy saved to that point.

Vermont has thirty-four aid stations, and I pick five for drop bags: mile 18, mile 44, mile 68, mile 84, and mile 90. The first four have a change of socks and shoes (foot care is as important as hydration, fuel, and electrolytes), and they all have energy drink mixed for my CamelBak and other necessities to the point of redundancy. If you don't need it, you'll get it back after you finish, but if you don't have it, you might DNF because it wasn't there.

A more experienced friend told me, "100 miles is easy, once you make it to mile 68, to meet your pacer." My friend John Dwyer agreed to accompany me for the last 32 miles. Formerly a 2:40 marathoner, John has a few dings from martial arts and hard use generally, and so has not been running in years. But he geared up for this, power-walking with a weight vest. I told him we'd probably walk most of the final piece anyway. From our many whitewater canoe adventures, I knew John would be resourceful if we had any trouble.

RD's Jim Hutchinson – Vt. 100; and
Michael Silverman – Vt. 50; Mt. Ascutney
in the background

Race director Jim Hutchinson kindly agreed to show John and me most of the last 32 miles of the course a few weeks beforehand. We power walked that section the following day, after a pleasant night in tents at Ascutney State Park. Familiarity with the course gave us a huge confidence boost.

For many ultrarunners, the 100 mile run is proof of legitimacy. Not that 100 mile veterans don't respect those 100k and 50 mile runners, but I still recall at Rocky Raccoon the century runner saying to us 50 milers, "So you're the folks going on the fun run?" We all know the rewards, the testing, the mind expansion, the thrill of the finish and the afterglow of accomplishment that ultrarunning provides, yet most will say the 100 yields proof of a mind's mettle beyond the scope of shorter distances.

So there's pressure in anticipation of the first 100. It's a high stakes proposition. With so much invested, there's a lot to lose if you don't finish. It wouldn't be failure so much as a carried threat, that if you did not try again and succeed, you might then have to look at it all as failure. Who likes threats or do-overs?

I worry about the night. Like most first timers, I've not run through the night before. Sleep has been a nighttime staple all my life. I've read about people getting "verrry" tired running through the night, people taking naps across the trail so the next runners coming along would trip over them and wake them up, runners who napped themselves out of the race altogether. Would I need sleep so much that I might fail? In the nights leading to the event, I lie in bed, rehearsing; sleeplessness is my biggest concern, more so than my physical ability to finish.

Right before the 4 a.m. start, fireworks and a tuxedoed piano player working the theme from "Chariots of Fire" get plenty of adrenalin flowing. The first few miles are dark, with uphill trails, before breaking onto the smooth packed dirt road that makes up 75% of the running surface.

With first light I settle, check my time at Densmore Hill (mile 3.8) and see I'm on pace. The aid stations have mileage posted on them, but I keep a list taped to the water bottle I carry to ensure good pace monitoring.

Taftsville covered bridge at mile 12 - Vermont 100.

After mile 12, there's a road crossing and the Taftsville covered bridge. It's another New England shrine for me (like Mount Washington's Tuckerman Ravine). I feel I belong right here, in this country I've crisscrossed so many times on ski, hiking, and canoe trips. Seeing this place brings inspirational remembrance of challenges past, in which I endured and reached goals I'd been wishing for.

Closing on Pomfret (mile 18), there's a delightful downhill on smooth wooded track - still morning cool with sunlight reaching through the trees to light the open spaces where I run. Magic. John greets me at mile 18 with the drop bag. I change socks and shoes, shirt and shorts, add fuel, take sunglasses, and scoot (takes probably 12 minutes). My opinion on aid station strategy is, know what you're going to do, execute efficiently, and don't worry about time. What you don't want is to forget something that can put you in trouble later because you were in a rush.

After Pomfret, there's quite a bit of trail climbing over the back of Suicide Six ski area, with spectacular views to reward the effort as you approach the top. Then quite a bit of downhill, mostly runnable. I plan to walk up ALL the hills and to run downhill as much as possible.

Now it's getting hotter. Temperatures reach into the mid 70's with intermittent cloud cover. July can be much hotter; we get a good break with the weather. Crossing over another shrine, Lincoln covered bridge (mile 36.1), I see kids playing in the clear river (oh, how tempting), but know I must stick to the matter at hand. Here's a guy with ski poles going along merrily, wanting to socialize. I'm determined to stay focused for the entire 100 miles, to waste no extra energy or allow distractions, so I pass him with a simple hello. At Vondell Reservoir (mile 32.7) I see my first drop, a guy with a knee problem. I suppose if one starts with an injury or feels iffy at all, chances are good he/she won't finish. I wonder why people feeling that way even bother. They must feel compelled, or fatalistic.

I'm on pace, approaching Camp 10 Bear (mile 44.2), where the medical people weigh me (same 182 as pre-race weigh in). I change again, add fuel, and take a bite of pb&j before going out at 3:30 p.m. About

½ mile out, here comes Jenny Capel (second place female finisher), heading towards her mile 68.2, a full 23 miles ahead of me. I do not indulge in this contrast as it could be demoralizing; this is my contest, not anyone else's.

I follow right turn markers onto a smaller road marked "Agony Hill." Soon I'm in a rutted, muddy, boulder strewn, bug infested climb, slowing to a workable pace. You take what the day gives you, and there's always time. This passes soon enough.

At Birmingham's (mile 51.7) I figure I've done the first 50 miles in about 13 hours. Back in the wooded trail, the persistent bowelly feeling I've carried since chugging a 350 calorie Boost nine hours ago needs attention. Mosquitoes have a feast, but I come out of the woods feeling lighter.

I'm tired, and I think of John meeting me in about three hours at the second 10 Bear (mile 68). All the planning, buying new gear, the training he's put in to this; I cannot let him down. John served in the Marines. I was Navy, to escape the bullets in Vietnam. To help prepare for this run, I read about SEALS, LRRPS, Spec Ops and other men in 'Nam, fighting the ultimate fight, deprived of sleep, "all giving some, some giving it all" for a cause they knew wasn't supported enough for them to win. My hardship here and now is but candlelight to those bonfires of dedication and will. This much I can do.

At Cox's (mile 60) there's a crowd of people having a good time, barbecue going and liquor on the table.

I take some ice and water, a pickle slice and a bite of grilled chicken, just for the taste, but I spit it out in caution that it could spur nausea. On this point, I had my best success ever combating nausea using crystallized ginger in combination with Tums, Rolaids, and E-Load (in the day's heat).

It's eight o'clock and getting cooler. I can move a little faster now, and while I've been getting behind pace a bit I start to make time back: 100k in 16 hours. At Brown School House (mile 62.8) the volunteer cautions on approaching dark and the rough trail ahead. I have a flashlight but pick up the pace on the uneven and gravelly trail to beat the dark as much as I can - slower when dark.

Back on the road, and it's dark, but I'm lit and walking up the hill, thinking I should make mile 68.2 about 9:30 p.m. Now down into the welcoming light of Camp 10 Bear, and there's John looking good to go. I weigh in again (184; up 2), change, take a ½ cheese sandwich and the best chicken noodle soup ever. New shoes are a full size larger; I notice my hands are swollen and surely my feet will need the extra room. Headlamp and fanny pack with extra clothes, chocolate covered espresso beans and Jolt caffeinated gum. We depart 10 Bear at 9:45.

Now up an uneven trail in the woods, but it's familiar to us and we're in a cheery mood. Back on the road at the top of the hill I suggest to John that we try to run the down slope. My body protests, so we go back to walking. No problem – our planned pace for this piece is 3 1/3 mph, so walking will do. I eat the beans and chew four pieces of Jolt, with Juicy Fruit to taste – a good wad.

I tell John I need to stop to empty pebbles from my shoes. A passing runner asks, "Everything OK?" I say I've collected all the pebbles from the road in my shoes and am pouring them out. He says thanks for taking them so others won't pick them up in their shoes. Such is the sense of nighttime thinking.

We come upon a runner who has stopped to wait for us. He's lost and says he's afraid of bears. He joins us. He's fidgety, moving his light all over and whistling. This disturbs the karma. As we reach Ashley (mile 81.9), a volunteer asks, "What can I get you?" to which our new companion responds, "Coffee, please," sitting down in a chair as if it were a diner. This doesn't sit with me, so I say, "We'll meet you at Bill's (mile 83.4)." The guy bolts out of his chair and hurries to join us, coffee be damned. I tell him bears are shy creatures, not very large, and would run the other way if met by a human. Ever the prankster, John says, "Well, they might be shy, but my cousin saw one over in Plymouth that was nine feet tall. But it's really the wild boars out here that you have to worry about at night. They aren't shy, and they will come right after you." "John," I whisper, "do you know what you're doing? Now we'll never lose 'Mr. Karmalost.'"

It's only 1½ miles, but from Ashley to Bill's it's uphill on uneven terrain and seems much longer. More Jolt gum. Bill's is a big station, with another weigh in (187; up 5 pounds; ibuprofen can cause fluid retention), more world's best chicken noodle soup, and very helpful volunteers. Change of socks and new fuel for the CamelBak and we're out of there, somehow without our erstwhile companion. Maybe he's asking someone about the wild boars - I don't know.

What I do know is I'm not sleepy, everything's working OK, and my redoubtable pacer is laughing about our lost ursus-phobe. We're in fine shape as we hit a paved road stretch just before the long climb up Blood Hill. Because we've done them before, Blood and Densmore Hills come under discussion: which is harder? We thought Densmore, but after completing it, Blood won out: it may be shorter, but it's a constant pitch, while Densmore has breaks in it. Up, up, and steeply up Blood we go.

It's after 4 a.m., and I begin to worry about our pace. "Hey, John, let's try running down the hills for a while." This goes well, and by the time we reach Jenneville (mile 90), my legs have come back to life. As we fuel up, I tell John, "Let's put the hammer down. It's a quarter to five, and we've got to hustle if we're going to beat 28 hours. I feel OK, and I want to finish with nothing left. Let's use it up." We drop all non-essentials that we've been carrying and run out of Jenneville.

So we walk up but run down the hills as they roll under our feet. I've switched to grape/cranberry juice, and it tastes great. I've got hot spots between the balls of my feet and stop to vaseline them, which helps a little. There's always time; it's worth it. The new day's light also triggers diurnal body mechanisms, and we gain energy. We guess how long it will take to crest Densmore Hill as we begin up, and forty minutes is about right. Now six miles to go, and we're running again.

We've made such good time from Jenneville that when we reach South Woodstock (mile 96.1), I see the chance to consider a reach under 27 hours. I consult with John: "If we can make 12 minute miles for the next four miles, we'll finish under 27." He says, "OK - if you want to try, I'm game." But that is too ambitious, given my condition and the hills that remain before us. After about 200 yards, I relent, "Let's forget that one but still go up tempo."

We're running, even some uphill sections. We pass about six people in the last four miles, sneaking up behind quietly, then bursting past, the way people do on training runs. Where does this energy come from? I marvel at it, running up a steep hill to pass another walker: "C'mon, John." (He's slowed to take his warmer shirt off.)

I'm possessed. I'm going to finish my first 100. Hints of sentimentality rise into my eyes, but I deny them; no, I will finish strong. I want to run through. John catches up, and I tell him we're going to finish together, no matter what. More trying uphills test us before we finally hear the cheers for finishing runners, beyond the next hill. I suggest, "Let's finish with an ultra shuffle, not a sprint, to show them what old hands we are." And so through in 27:12 to desultory cheers from a few bleary eyed finish line officials. It's 7:15 a.m.; how about a shower and some breakfast?

And so we do. Sitting in a booth at The Creamery in Wooodstock, John and I can't stop repeating what a smooth go we had, and how well we feel in front of a large plate of eggs, potatoes, and hash. More coffee, please.

Late Sunday morning, John and I part ways: he to New Jersey, me to Boston. After about twenty minutes on the road, I'm overcome with drowsiness, the car drifting dangerously. I try to intensify my focus, but again the car veers onto the gravel shoulder. I jerk the wheel to correct back to the pavement, thinking, "I can't drive like this." I exit the highway, find a rest area, nap for an hour, then make it safely home.

Later that afternoon when my family comes back from Maine, they find me in bed. "What's the matter, Mike? Are you feeling OK? You never take naps," Deedie inquires. "I feel great," I reply. "I just ran 100 miles."

Seeing that I'm not hurt, Deedie offers congratulations.

———

START ME UP

Two months after Vermont, I ran the Mount Pisgah 50k, a classic New England trail run in southern New Hampshire. Pisgah was on a wish list of ultramarathons I'd researched on the internet.

There, I tried my first pair of trail running shoes from Montrail (after breaking them in beforehand), and what a difference they gave. Over rooted and rocky terrain, the stiffer soles made a more stable platform that allowed me to run faster, and the reinforced toe box protected my toes from the contusions I had come to accept as part of the price admission to the trail running experience. My somewhat masochistic tough-guy self image was changing to accommodate improved technologies: from equipment to nutrition to supplements. I was learning how to enjoy not punishing myself. Soon after Pisgah, I ordered toe socks from Injinji, which in combination with trail shoes effectively put an end to bloody toes and multiple toenail loss.

I applied for the Western States 100 lottery (lottery because of its popularity) that fall. Western States is the granddaddy of all the 100 mile events, and I figured I should try it. When I got news in December that I'd failed to win a place for 'States in 2004, I went back to my wish list and plan B.

———

HOLIDAY LAKE 50+K
February 4, 2004

Every ultrarunner should meet David Horton, one of our living legends: he ran the 2650 mile Pacific

Crest Trail in 67 days, averaging over 40 miles per day, and still holds that record. I went from Boston to Appomattox for the ninth running of the Holiday Lake 34.5 mile run, where David's the RD. East coasters and Midwesterners find this event's February placement on the calendar convenient for gearing up toward the peak running months of summer/fall.

Bending my rule of not traveling far for a 50k, I rationalized: this is one event I have to do to for a more complete ultra experience. A little farmland, possum, bible, Civil War remembrance, and mid-winter ultrarunner socialization with David presiding seemed an exceptional opportunity I couldn't pass up.

———

The Friday night dinner is one of the better pre-run pasta feeds you'll find, as David thoughtfully enhances congeniality by providing name tags. There, I would meet new people and identify faces with names.

Through a frigid January I weighed imponderables such as why I grind my teeth at night, why I drive like a madman, is perfection worth chasing, and why running long in companionship with others brings me closer to the answers. The Mt. Pisgah 50k last September seems a long way back, and my psyche needs an ultra fix: it's a New Year and a new running season.

David Horton and Bethany (Hunter) Patterson.

Interpolating results and rating the condition I'm in, I come up with 6 ½ hours as the goal. This will make a good training run for Grasslands 50 miler in March, which should make a good training run for the Kettle Moraine 100 miler in June. For me they're all training runs; I'm too slow to race. The point is just to finish, possibly with some incremental cognitive gain on why I grind my teeth at night, etc. Only, I don't want to learn so much about myself that I lose the desire to continue running.

Holiday Lake is an entirely runnable loop done twice, the second loop in reverse. Each loop is just over 17 miles. It's mostly single track for two plus miles, then jeep road, then single track for three plus miles to the start/finish, then back.

There are two soaking stream crossings done twice. It's a younger average age group with several first timers. Many people run side by side in the jeep tracks swapping run stories. Temperatures typically go from freezing into the high forties.

I find that weight training – medium weight and high reps – helps my endurance in the second half. I run reverse splits (the second half being faster than the first half), thanks to good cardio reserves that seem deeper than usual, after just 2 ½ months in the weight room. And there's the "two hour window," the estimated time remaining that when reached, gives me the green light to open up to full throttle, through to the finish. The trick is to pace conservatively up to that point. Though it's not a race, it's exhilarating to pass people, isn't it?

What's a "Horton mile"? I'm running a nine minute mile pace, just less than twenty minutes from the finish, when volunteer Bethany Hunter cruises past me going out to encourage back of the packers: "Good job," she says, "You're a little over one mile from the finish." Pressing hard, I finish 6 hours, 25 minutes. Thanks, David; it's a pleasure to know you.

———

GRASSLANDS 50 MILER
March 20, 2004

I picked Grasslands, near Dallas, because it's an early season 50 miler and to meet Suzi Cope, one of our legends. Her story in *Running Through the Wall*... inspired me; she tells of running the Massanutten 100 miler, having declared beforehand that it would be her last. After a long, distinguished history of ultrarunning experiences, Suzi offers a fine lesson in self-knowledge, and in accepting the inevitable consequence of what is age appropriate.

From fifteen degree Boston winter training runs I went to an eighty-six degree, bright scorcher of a Texas day. The Grasslands course has long stretches of sand. Suzi relates that if there's moisture in the ground, the sand firms up and makes for good running. In 2004, I found the dry, deep sand stretches very tough to deal with. I went out at a forcing pace in the cool morning, and the fast onset of heat took me by surprise. By the time I felt it, it was too late to recover. I tried lots of fluids, ice packs on my neck, electrolytes – everything I could think of – but I was already cooked; I dropped out after only twenty-eight miles.

Did Not Finish is so pathetic, most race directors mercifully do not include these folks in the results they post, following the event. Non-finishers carry anonymous shame until they redeem their loss with a finish. DNF is a tough reminder that you can't "just show up" and expect to have a good result.

REPAIR SHOP

After Grasslands, I go through some serious soul-searching. Did I go to Texas too confident, not trained up enough? Did Grasslands signal burn out; should I let running go, is my life out of balance? Can I leave that Vermont 100 finish alone there – a one time wonder – or should I take Grasslands as a signal that if I want to continue this magnificent journey of life discovery, I will have to take training and preparation more seriously?

I treat it like a physical injury, starting up again with short, technically focused runs, working on the fundamental stride, breathing right, good diet, plenty of sleep, and renewed commitment to my relationship with Deedie. She's beginning to understand that ultrarunning for me is a rebuilding process, that it establishes the security in the wild I'd long hoped to find. I tell her I believe what I'm doing is good for us; she's not convinced, but she doesn't object any more. We vacation in Florida, walking the beach, holding hands, small talking or not talking at all. We show appreciation for each other. After more than twenty years, it's easy to take too much for granted, easy to forget how important the little things are. We rekindle there, in gentle accommodation of occasionally opposing wills for ourselves, and for each other.

———

A month later, I'm at Lake Waramaug in Connecticut. Every April, this low key event offers 50k, 50 mile, and 100k distances, done in 7 mile road loops around the lake, in a gentle country setting. Waramaug is a good way for a marathoner moving up to try the 50k distance without having to deal with the added difficulty of trail running.

Aid station volunteers at Lake Waramaug make sure runners get enough to eat and drink

Though my plan to ramp up for Kettle Moraine in June has been smudged by the Grasslands experience, I figure a good 50k run here can begin the concentrated part of training for my second 100 miler. Waramaug goes well, a solid 5:25 finish.

More experienced 100 milers advise that the training cycle should include a sustained period of consistently high mileage with a longer taper before the event. I put in three consecutive 60+ mile weeks, including long back-to-backs on weekends and 30 miles at the G.A.C. Mother's Day 6 hour event (Topsfield, Ma.) to finish the long run part of my training cycle. In the three weeks before Kettle, I back mileage down to 30, then 20, then 10, with more up tempo fartlek sessions. Many people put in much higher mileage to train for 100's, and a few do less than I; the primary training objective is to become confident that you can complete 100 miles in whatever way works for you.

———

KETTLE MORAINE 100 MILE RUN

June 4, 2004

The Kettle Moraine endurance runs happen in early June in south central Wisconsin. In 2004, 103 contestants enter the 100 miler, with an additional 38 people in relay teams, and 46 in the 100k. RD's Tim Yanacheck and Jason Dorgan provide excellent organization in a relaxed and cheerful manner, which helps soothe pre-event jitters.

Under the start/finish banner just before the 6 a.m. start, I feel a wave of anticipation, near anxiety in the flashing enormity of what I am about to do. In an impulse I cover my face with my hands, take a deep breath, then murmur, "Congratulations, now go forth and scribble."

These were K's words on being sent to war in Alexandra Fuller's fine new book, *Scribbling the Cat*. I train for ultras not just physically but also by reading what I can find to stiffen my will. Along with several other books on war I also read Joe Simpson's *The Beckoning Silence* and Scott Tinley's *Racing the Sunset*. Knowing that these people triumphed over intense physical challenges makes accepting my challenge here a bit easier.

The course is 100% trail and nearly all runnable. The first 7 ½ miles lead to a 23 ½ mile easterly route to the 31 mile turnaround. Runners reverse course to the start/finish, repeat the 7 ½ mile leg back out, then turn west 11 ½ miles to a turnaround and reverse that part to the finish. The 100 mile event has a low completion history, not for the difficulty of terrain, but because when people reach the start/finish after 62 miles, the temptation to call it a day looms large. There are a lot of small hills in the 7 ½ mile section, which can become a gauntlet when you know you must face them a third and fourth time.

Studying split times from the 2003 event, I set a pace objective accordingly: 16 miles in 3 ½ hours, turnaround in 7, 100k in 15 ½, the final 38 miles in 12 ½, for a 28 hour goal.

Joe Prusaitis once told me he can look into people's eyes at the start of a 100 miler and tell who's not going to finish. Because I'm convinced you have to be completely committed to finishing well before the start and must maintain a 100% positive attitude throughout the effort, I don't seek out doubting eyes, but I know they are here. For those moments of struggle along the way, I hold two thoughts from the Massanuten 100 reports I've read just days before: if you're thinking of dropping, ask yourself: "Since you're here, what else would you do today, anyway?" and remember: the cumulative experience of prior ultra runs will provide resources to draw from when you need them.

I hold another trump card: my daughter Lila and her friend Carly have agreed to greet me at the 31 mile turnaround, then accompany me through the night from mile 62 to mile 81 (the Rice Lake turnaround). We're a team, so in the three or four times I consider dropping out, I remember that I cannot allow myself to let them down. This proves huge and certainly makes it easier for me to endure through to the finish.

I make the 16 mile aid station on pace but find the day's heat in open sections puts me behind when I reach the aid station at mile 26. So I put the hammer down a bit in order to reach mile 31 at 1 p.m. as planned with my pacers. Now passing many runners, I wonder if my pace is too aggressive. Will this haunt me later on?

Confidence flows when I see Lila and Carly at Scuppernong (mile 31). Quick change of shirt, socks and shoes, and out: "See you at the 100k around 9:30 tonight." Their cheerful encouragement gives me strength.

Temperatures rise to the mid 70's. Partial cloud cover and a slight breeze lighten the heat load as I flow back through open country. But something about the combination of a turkey sandwich and tea with Spiz (a high calorie energy mix) from my CamelBak brings on nausea. I try ginger and Tums but still feel like hurling. Should I let go? I weigh the adverse result of fuel depletion from hurling versus the discomfort and slower pace from not hurling. I accept the regurgitating reflex, but somehow my system holds steady, and I plod on.

Now reaching the final 7 ½ mile stretch leading to the 100k turnaround, I see that I need to go up tempo again to make my 9:30 p.m. estimate. While I know this risks burnout, I remind myself, "From the turnaround we'll be walking and I can recover then." Darkness envelops the scene, and I put on my flashlight. Many 100 milers pass on their way back out, and I have to remember it's their race, not mine: this slower pace is right for me.

Soon I'm into the start/finish where Lila and Carly look to me like two fresh horses ready to bolt. Change of shirt, socks and shoes, fanny pack with night gear, headlamp, and – wow – Ramen noodle soup, a welcome change from pb&j quarters and that unsettling turkey sandwich.

The team heads out: Lila and Carly lit up with excitement, me with a Ramen rush. I set the pace for a mile or two, then ask them to lead; following allows

Kettle Moraine's gentle forest floor makes an
easy running surface.

me to move mechanically without having to think
much. We discuss pace, and I assure them that just
walking this way, we'll stay on plan. We use green
lights, which I much prefer, as they soften contrast
and cast a gentler presentation underfoot.

For 6 ½ hours we go along, Carly and Lila chatting
occasionally, while I draft in their energy. When we
make the Highway 12 (mile 77) aid station at 3 a.m.,
someone says Smarty Jones lost the Belmont Stakes
and Ronald Reagan died.

So wonderfully out of place, this news. We run long distances to disengage from things of this world, so when we return to them, our perspective is less needy.

From Highway 12 to Rice Lake, terrain is rockier with more short hills and several sets of stairs set apart in such a way to make your quads bark. Good stuff. Knowing Lila and Carly have the car waiting at the turnaround, the bad angels begin to ask me, how will I tell my pacers I'm going to pack it in after 81 miles? Negative thoughts tempt me. Then Lila asks, "Dad, how long do you think it will take you to get to the finish from here?" Inspiring question. And, "How do you feel?" I respond, "I'm tired, but I think I'll finish around 11:20 a.m."

I leave a big cushion versus plan for the remaining 19 miles, because I'm so very tired. You never know how much the new day will bring up energy reserves. It's 4:20 a.m. We say goodbye to each other; they head for some shut-eye, and I go back to the rocks, hills and stairs. I'm proud of them, so grateful they are here to help me. I feel waves of emotion and confidence and purpose, figuring, "Just another six hours, and I'll be done."

Creeping dawn comes slowly, as there's overcast and drizzle, but just after 5 a.m., I put my lights away. Reaching the mile 85 aid station a few minutes before 6 a.m., I go with more Ramen noodles, orange quarters in the pocket and the stimulating thought that I'll be able to see the ground we covered last night, as I return. I feel physically disengaged, mind holding body like a puppet on strings. It's going well.

I knock my head on a tree branch around mile 87, the same branch I knocked my head on going out – not so hard to hurt, just more of an amusing wake-up. Now through regimentally planted pines, perfectly spaced, seeming unnatural. I stop to clear a shoe, struggling to sit. Mosquitoes swarm, so recently hatched they don't yet have penetrating power – a day later and I'd be throwing a blood and itch party. Ahead I see another 100 miler, walking stiffly, arms nearly rigid, not a pretty sight. I pass, offering words of encouragement.

Just before 8 a.m., I approach the mile 92.5 aid station. A volunteer appears, asking, "How many are behind you?" "Three or four," I reply. "They dropped, so you're probably the last one," he says. This doesn't sit well with me, as finishing is one thing, but finishing last is quite another. I take some delicious cut fruit in a cup and coffee in another, seeing that I've got just less than 2 hours to make a 28 hour finish. Good 'ol adrenalin starts to flow, as I know I can run two hours anytime, anywhere.

Ahead I see competitors walking. I can take them. Zombies. Dawn of the living dead. I think, "Open the throttle and throw yourself at the hills." And I do. I love this part, when you can smell the barn and you run holding nothing back. There is nowhere else I'd rather be than right here, right now, blowing doors off and blowing gaskets. My heart jumps at me in protest, and I have to throttle back. I want to finish strong, but

I also want to finish to run another day. Wheedling the red line is great, great, great.

After surmounting more hills than I can remember or count, I see the trail flatten out and hear cars on the road near the finish. It seems so very long, that last mile or so, but I'm running, dammit, and I will break 28 hours. Oh, deliverance. Up a little rise, and I come to an undefined finish point, where Tim emerges saying, "Just stop anywhere; this is it." In a chair there, I see a fellow who's obviously also just finished. He looks me straight and deep in the eyes, wanting to see again for himself what it's like. I recognize him, my brother, and myself in him, as our eyes lock and broad smiles wash over us both.

I did not do this alone: thanks Tim, thanks Jason, and thanks to all the volunteers who worked tirelessly to help us fulfill our dreams. Most of all, thanks to you, Lila and Carly, for your wonderful support and inspiration.

———

CHAPTER FIVE – LOSING BAGGAGE

Finishing one 100 miler, I could remember the experience of visiting beyond previously imagined personal limits. Finishing a second 100 miler, I began to live outside that envelope. Little everyday bothers became trivial; bigger issues like personal relationships and career decisions had clearer paths to solution. I found more patience. I understood the benefits of problem solving, in contrast to the discouragement of problem avoidance. Engagement with reality took me across those finish lines, not complaining, not self-pitying, not pretending. I came to know my pace and rhythm in training and held onto them for 100 miles, twice. I knew how to address my present and future needs and how to extend beyond the reach of my body's crying. I met the person I always wanted to be but never thought possible. It was all there; I wanted more.

Following Kettle, I enjoyed several weeks of unstructured, light exercise to recover. A persistent stiffness in my neck would not respond to usually effective treatments, not even massage. I went to a Rolfing specialist, for deep (and painful) tissue manipulation. As I listened to his holistic talk about stress, diet, breathing, and posture, I saw that while I might now be living outside the envelope of formerly perceived limitations, I was still captive within my own body's habitual, protective responses to unconscious, emotional disquiet. I asked him if he could fix my stiff neck. He said he couldn't, that I was the only one who could, by more consciously integrating mind and body practices until they became automatically linked in a de-stressed, free-swinging self. I felt like the Tin Man in *The Wizard of Oz*. Realizing that Rolfing treats the symptoms of physical discomfort and not the causes, I said goodbye to the Rolfing man and began to look for mind/body integration in the study of yoga, zen, and Buddhist philosophy.

Vermont 50 finish, lower left,
as seen from Mt. Ascutney.

I took my stiff neck in late September to run the Vermont 50 mile trail event at Mount Ascutney. This one includes bicycles as well as runners, for either 50 kilometer or 50 mile distances, over tough trails and hills. After an equipment change at the 32 mile aid station, I missed a turn while straightening out my CamelBak, cutting off about three miles before re-joining runners on the correct trail. It became my Vermont 47 mile trail run from that point to a disappointing finish. Driving home, I saw a spectacular sunset reflection on Mount Sunapee (New Hampshire). At that moment, the zen adage "When chopping wood, only chop wood" came to me, and I understood why I had missed that turn. Distractions in minds not trained to dismiss them result in a conflicted mind/body connection, where purposes are forgotten, misdirection is frequent, and accidents happen.

I took my Vermont screw-up and my stiff neck in October to the Cape Cod Marathon, my third consecutive finish, all within four minutes of each other. Then in November I made a day trip to the Rhode Island Nifty Fifty road events, for the 50k option (now it's 50 miles only). This is another New England road loop classic that would make a nice first 50 miler for anyone not ready for the added difficulty of trail running. I finished without getting lost and wrapped up the 2004 season, realizing I had a new kind of work to do if I was going to take running and myself to the next level.

———

MIND TRAINING

The Catholic priest sex predator scandal extinguished what little remaining spiritual investment I had in the Church. In my day, I'd been queered by a Christian Brother college guidance counselor. Now I knew that for centuries, all over the world, so many people holding the power of religious leverage had been ruining the lives of innocents, driven themselves by blatantly uncontrollable, hurtful desires.

In my religious education, I'd become hardwired to feel right and wrong, duty, sacrifice, and especially guilt from sinning against the rules of the Church and its God. What an unbelievable, chaotic fix I was in, that my parents and their parents were put in; good intentions now morphed into ghastly haunting regret and sadness, as I contemplated my religious background in this new light. And with the scandal finally made public, widespread denial issued forth from the "faithful," who tut-tutted that it was the doing of only a few. I saw instead the recurrence of systemic, human self-destruction – similar to past wars waged against the infidel, Church sponsored killing and maiming of innocents – god, how horrible. And Christians are not the only zealots who propagate the contradiction of human hurt, wearing the mask of virtuous purpose.

My stiff neck was symptomatic of a carried stress that bad karma put into me. I did not blame my parents, or the Catholic Church, or myself. I just knew I had to get my head straight, or I'd continue to pass the stress of a conflicted mind into my body, thereby limiting its potential range and power. Trail runners trip and fall because they're distracted; with better focus they can maintain balance and more easily envision the next series of foot placements. Such distractions run very deep, below conscious thinking.

Running 50 miles and longer, I had consistently gone through the barrier of body over mind to the "other side" of mind over body. The point of departure forces the body to loosen its grip and get behind the mind's power instead of standing in the way of it, as is typically the case. Breaking through the barrier again and again, I found that I kept more and more of the feeling of mind power after each long run.

I wanted to find out how to hold constant mind power, more focus without distraction, consistently in everyday doings. Ultrarunning's great gift that I did not anticipate when I started going long now came clear to me: it's experiencing and keeping the Magic I heard about when I first was at Catalina. Every ultra runner meets the Magic. Few are able to describe what it means to them, but that doesn't diminish the strength that it carries.

Buddhist thinking says a person benefits in working away from id, ego, and superego: the "I, me, mine" mentality most people are stuck with. It's the only way to develop independent thinking. I'm not Buddhist and don't want to be one, but I like the way they think. Some distractions come simply from physical surroundings, others from inside the mind – dreamlike – in its ever busy, unconscious effort to reconcile conflicted thought or being. Many unconscious conflicts derive from preconceived, planted judgments or ideas that people – parents, teachers, authority figures – put into our minds, not truly our own judgments or ideas. They fit uncomfortably, like someone else's clothing.

Running through the point of departure frees the mind from the body's needy, complaining drag; so too, I imagined, it's possible for me to break mentally free, when I choose, from everyday judgments or emotional attachments, which on first thought seem simply part of who I am, but on deeper reflection I see as impediments (from the Latin, "impedimenta," or "baggage") to original thinking.

As part of my training, I took 40 minute walks, counting breath cycles with my footsteps – at first four steps inhaling, four steps exhaling, then six, then eight, then ten steps to inhale and ten to exhale slowly, working into mind/body integration. I ran the Hyannis Marathon in February, then the Lake Waramaug 50k and the Mother's Day 6 hour events again, same as the previous year. Waramaug went a little slower, but I added another mile in the 6 hour event to make 31 miles this time. I ran with focus on breathing rhythm, moving more freely and with more efficiency in my stride. I sensed more control over the release of my energy stores and more relaxation while running. The stiff neck left me.

I picked up *The Universe in a Single Atom* by the Dalai Lama in which he introduces the Buddhist philosophy of emptiness. This seemed similar to my experiences of running past the point of departure. He writes: "One of the most philosophical insights in Buddhism comes from what is known as the theory of emptiness. At its heart is the deep recognition that there is a fundamental disparity between the way we perceive the world, including our own existence in it, and the way things actually are. In our day-to-day experience, we tend to relate to the world and to ourselves as if these entities possess self-enclosed, definable, discrete, and enduring reality. For instance, if we examine our own concept of selfhood, we will find that we tend to believe in the presence of an essential core to our being, which characterizes our individuality and identity as a discrete ego, independent of the physical and mental elements that constitute our existence. The philosophy of emptiness reveals that this is not only a fundamental error but also the basis for attachment, clinging, and the development of our numerous prejudices."

That's it! I seized this connection like a hound on a scent.

———

LAUREL HIGHLANDS – APPROACHES TO GOD
June 11, 2005

Catharine sees me first near the baggage claim where we arranged to meet. We hug in a clutter of backpacks and papers with directions to our destination, Laurel Highlands. Months in planning, this adventure is framed in hard training, hope, and trust.

The Laurel Highlands 70.5 mile trail run happens every June in southwestern Pennsylvania. Catharine, my goddaughter, will pace me from mile 46 to the end. This will be her first ultrarunning experience. Months back, her Dad, my good friend Dick, told me she'd be interested in participating; now we're here, brimming with anticipation.

I'm still working to become an accomplished ultrarunner, more eager to pose as one than I realize. I've completed two 100 mile events, but I'm not ready yet to try one alone. I'm hoping Catharine might become a willing pacer for a third 100 that I plan to run in the fall. Laurel Highlands will offer us the chance to evaluate this prospect.

Catharine's been training in Santa Fe. In our e-mail correspondence she describes grand landscapes seen from altitude, single track trails through cactus and sand, vivid colors from distant desert vistas.

What will happen? I feel like some mixture of a Dad and a guy on a blind date. And Catharine – is this 24 year old anxious when thinking about an up close and personal weekend with a 58 year old man she doesn't know very well? It's exciting, it's different, it's upon us.

Doubt creeps when we discover her baggage didn't make it. It's Friday at 5 p.m., and the start's on Saturday at 5:30 a.m. It's an hour and a half drive to our cabin. We need time to organize gear, make a fine meal, relax, catch up, and get a good night's sleep. Instead, the confidence that a planned time line brings is lost.

Now we're in a cavernous sporting goods store, looking for new running equipment. It seems interminably long for her to decide which shoes to buy.

I begin to realize the game plan is changing but that I have to go with it if we're going to have a chance to make something of the weekend. During the drive to Seven Springs I share with Catharine my intellectual curiosity in why people enjoy ultrarunning. In the book *Why God Won't Go Away*, the authors write that long distance running is one of several different observed practices that cause changes in brain activity, similar to meditation or prayer, thereby setting a platform for departure into a realm of expanded consciousness. This consciousness brings one closer to a presence in the myth of immortality, or oneness with an eternal being. I explain that as a non-practicing Christian, I'm curious to explore scientific reasoning as to why people are religious; in this way I might be able to circle back to my childhood and understand why my parents put religion into my life. Ultrarunning has given me moments of spirituality that feel more "religious" than the conventional practices of earlier years. I want to understand more about all of this.

Catharine listens behind dark glasses.

We're at the start now. It's dark, foggy and very warm. I don't feel as rested as I'd like, but I'm happy to extend the care and attention that I feel Catharine's companionship requires. I have three daughters close to her age, and while I'm not expert in understanding the female mind, I've developed a certain approach that seems to work, though it requires added effort.

I picked Laurel Highlands because it's tough. If I could complete this run, I would be ready for the Superior 100 miler, which is of comparable difficulty. There are forty-one 100 mile events every year around the country. I'm at a level where the 100 mile distance is my objective once a year. Many are mountainous or so challenging I can't imagine I'd have a shot at completing them. The two I've done so far, Vermont and Kettle Moraine, are rated among the easiest. Now I'm looking for something more challenging.

Laurel has four checkpoints runners have to make by a certain elapsed time if they're going to be allowed to continue. Catharine will meet me at checkpoint three, where the cut off is 7:30 p.m.

I make the earlier cut offs, each with 35 minutes to spare, despite sapping heat and a period of heavy rain that turns sections of the trail into a river of mud. Other parts are so rocky I have to pick my way through at a walking pace. In looking down for safe footing, I go off the trail two times onto other trails, for what they call "bonus miles," retracing my steps to get it right, while time ticked away. This isn't my best showing, but it's the best I can do. Putting all of that together, I'm pretty whipped when I meet Catharine at 7:08 p.m., but not ready to admit it.

Catharine's invested in this adventure also – months of training, planning, and traveling to be here. She's eager to see me after waiting so long. I'm distressed that I have so little energy left, but I must go on. So at mile 46 I head straight to my drop bag for new clothes and shoes, a little food, headlamp and flashlights for the night. We leave together for the long awaited last segment of the run, 24 miles with just over seven hours' time left.

I hope I'll find rejuvenation with her, now that the remaining distance is not so daunting. In previous runs, I'd been through bad patches that went away, somehow finding new energy. We rate our progress with our watches as we pass the mile markers, do the math, and realize that time is outrunning us (well, me, not Catharine) to the next checkpoint. Neither of us says what we know to be true, that we will not make it past the cut off time to the finish line. We continue on in darkness, silent at first. We begin to talk, Catharine initiating mostly, as I feel very tired and a little ashamed. She knows, I can tell, I am not now the person I claimed and want to be – this is our disappointing reality. I'm relieved she doesn't challenge me, as she might. In unspoken acceptance we begin to chat inquisitively about each other and the people in our lives.

We make the final checkpoint, mile 57, at 11:20 p.m., about 30 minutes past the cut off time. Game Over. After a shuttle to the finish, collecting gear and finding the car, we arrive at the motel around 2 a.m. and go directly to our rooms for a few hours' sleep.

Sunday morning on the way to the airport, we talk more about ourselves and the people in our lives. Catharine reminds me I told her on the way out that I'm not religious. She relates when she told friends in Santa Fe she was going on an ultra run with her godfather, they asked, "What's a godfather?" She repeats the question to me, "What is a godfather, Mike?" I think she knows but wants to hear what I will say. In my set Catholic literal truthfulness I answer: "In past times parents would select friends who were religious to be godparents, so that if anything should happen to them, their children would receive a religious education." Then I realize the box I've put myself in. If I'm not religious, how can I pretend to be Catharine's godfather? Even if completing Laurel Highlands could be weighed as a natural or secular religious experience, I haven't shown her that, either. In short order, in less than twelve hour's time, Catharine has unmasked me twice.

When we part, she throws a hug around me. Our eyes meet and hold there not quite long enough for me to gather what she's thinking, but it looks like, "Well, it's over now, and I'm moving on."

Catharine cares about certain "old goats," too.

And she does: four months later, Catharine runs her first marathon in Chicago with her sister Elizabeth. She sends me pictures of the two of them, wrapped in space blankets, looking proud.

———

In sports and in life, I've learned that never giving up or accepting defeat pays dividends. Such a mindset helps maintain the positive attitude that there's always a chance for improvement, there's always a next time. I got cooked at Laurel Highlands. From that I understood that attempting the Superior 100 miler would be completely unrealistic (having read all the personal accounts I could find, each one describing the event's difficulty). But my exciting life pilgrimage had to go on. Looking back, I saw several different persons in myself, from past to present: an arrogant alcoholic; an arrogant non-alcoholic; someone who sees that identity is not wealth or status but remains attached to them; someone who knows that needless attachments, or baggage, create internal conflict, thereby inhibiting potential for maximum performance and peace of mind; someone here and now, invested in ultrarunning as the practice that is changing me into the honest person I want to be. The wilderness I imagined in which comfort can't be bought partly existed in my unwitting alienation from others, created in selfishness. I have been an enemy to myself. Now, the self-sufficiency I have long yearned for seems reachable, as I find my way out of that wilderness. I'm struck with this irony: long periods of solitude while running ultramarathons are making me more sociable.

———

WAKELY DAM 32.6 MILE TRAIL RUN
July 23, 2005

Wakely RD Jim Houghtaling

Wakely Dam run hopefuls get a chance to enter by e-mail about six months in advance. Former Wakely runners get first crack at the very limited (by the Park service) field, and first timers go into a lottery for what few spots remain. I got in for 2005, and therefore felt I had to run Wakely for its unique challenges and for future year invites. It went like this:

Three thirty-eight a.m., I'm lying in the tent, eyes wide open, thinking, COFFEE.

Out in the dark with headlamp, I light the small propane burner for a boil and brew up. Holding the coffee in both hands, stocking hat in the folding chair, I stare at a billion stars, a soulful pale full moon and the twinkling water of Lake Piseco. They seem to whisper: "Today is going to be a good run."

Wakely Dam runners are good to
go 32 miles unsupported.

Before the start, forty-five charged-up runners shift about for a picture. A few words from Jim H. the RD, and we're off for Wakely Dam, 32.6 miles up the trail. The Northville-Placid Trail (NPT) runs 120 miles mostly north/south in New York State's Adirondack Park – they claim it's the largest state park in the 50 states. This run is unassisted, as in BYO. No crossroads, no aid stations; what you need, you bring with you. I have a 70 oz. CamelBak loaded with 800 calories of Spiz powder mixed in water on ice, a hand held 24 oz. bottle with more of the same, and another hand held with green tea on ice. My fanny pack contains five boiled potatoes in salt, orzo made with chicken broth in a 12 oz. nalgene bottle, a ProBar, three flasks of Hammer Gel, a bottle with M&M's, ziploc bags with ginger pieces, electrolyte tabs, ibuprofen, and iodine tabs for water scooped up along the way, an extra pair of socks and bungwad, handkerchief, desert hat with cape and desert shirt to keep nasty deer flies from sucking blood, and full length tights.

After the DNF at Laurel Highlands, I'm humbled, hungry, and hopeful. I plan to work the NPT with full concentration and my finest speed, consistent with the rolling judgment of conserving energy to allow a strong finish. The trail is technical, with fewer rocks and roots than Laurel Highlands, but with much arboreal blow down that forces circuitous re-routing through thickety woods to regain the trail proper. Some fallen trees can be stooped under, some climbed over. There's ample mud in places, with plank crossings through foot sucking marshy areas that can be avoided by skipping on rock tops or stepping on bushes.

Nearly all of it is runnable; knowing my limits, I walk most of the hills. But for looking down to good foot placement, there's great scenery. I miss most of it in survival instinct. I take two diggers, neither one hard. This run gives me another chance to exercise conscious breathing cycles that help propel me more efficiently and with greater relaxation. At one spot I'm cruising in a higher gear, breathing rhythmically, thinking how fine it all is when I get clothes lined by a fallen tree at head height. I fail to see it because I'm looking down - no blood, but a nice bruising raspberry on my chin, thank you very much.

Just beyond mile 16 I see I'm several minutes behind my planned eight hour finishing pace, but think that's OK. On account of all the fallen trees, I'm going as well as expected. I make two water stops: one at mile 13 where both hand held bottles get replenished and I begin fueling from the CamelBak, and the second at mile 23 from a spring coming out from under a poplar tree, where I fill only one hand held. At about mile 20 the CamelBak is dry, and I load it from the two hand helds, now purified. I will finish with no water left, according to plan.

In mile 27 I come upon a park ranger who reassures me I'm still on the NPT (follow the blue markers on trees) and it's 5.7 miles to the dam. The barn smell is palpable, and I step up the pace. I'm running up most of the hills now. The last two miles are on a dirt road, and I'm going as hard as I can across the Wakely bridge to the finish.

Yes, yes, yes.

My time of 8:33 is slower than I'd hoped, but a 67th percentile finishing place is well within my historical range of 50% to 80%. I'm happy with this. I drive home that afternoon – a two day round trip of 525 miles in the car, 32.6 miles running unassisted through the woods, a lousy sleep in the tent, and finally, a restful sleep in my own bed.

———

Now it's near the end of July, and I'm looking to October, for either the Heartland 100, an unpaved road out and back scheme in Kansas, or the Arkansas Traveller trail 100 in the Ouachita forest, about 30 miles west of Little Rock. After reading about each of them, I opt for the trail run, thinking when I'm older I can try the easier Heartland course (it has faster finishing times).

One of my long training runs in early August takes me to the top of Cadillac Mountain, on Mount Desert Island in Maine. The trail approach is rocky and steep. Nearing the summit I enter a cloud hanging there. Slowing in the dense fog and drizzle, I strain to see cairns marking the way. There's light rain and wind, with penetrating cold. I am not prepared for this. Hypothermia lurks, and I move more quickly to raise body temperature. This is problem solving. The other problem – where's the top of friggin' Cadillac? Suddenly, I see a pickup truck straight in front of me (from another approach, people can drive in comfort to the top). The park ranger inside cracks his window open, wipers beating furiously, and tells me, "Yep, this is it." My words of thanks to him fall into the truck's heated cab. I turn back down, now shivering, and choose a steeper, quicker route to the warmth I badly need. Broad granite rock faces tilting at an angle carry painted blue dash marks to show the way. Now wet, they're dangerously slippery. I need three or four contact points - any hand hold will do; a crack in the rock, a scrub pine bush, or just hope. One slip means ugliness. With slow, light steps I scuttle from safe point across danger to safe point, getting warmer as I descend. Finally down on the flats, in the wrap of security, I run home, thinking, "That was a fright. Next time, I'll carry the extra gear I could have used this time."

CONQUER THE CANUCK 92.2K
CRABBE MOUNTAIN
NEW BRUNSWICK, CANADA
Aug. 27-28, 2005

Number 2: "It's going to be hot today."

Number 5: "Yeah - could go up to 29."

I'm at the start of the inaugural Crabbe Mountain Conquer the Canuck event, 50k today and 42.2k tomorrow. Seven have entered the two-day stage run, with an additional five looking to run the 50k only.

My kind of event – small, remote, scenic. RD Roy Nicholl offers a brief course description as we follow on the maps he's given us. From the mid-mountain start/finish, we descend through cross-country ski trails to a stretch of gravel road, then through woods again to climb the 853' mountain, and down to the start/finish: twice, to make 50k.

I figure this might take six hours of easy running the first day, then five the next for the marathon. Forget it! Making the first loop in just under four hours, I see this will be much tougher than I thought.

Roy has made up signs like "Middle of Nowhere," "Gnarly Section," and "Piste de Resistance" (for the hill climb), placed in various locations for comic effect. I enjoy being in the middle of nowhere twice in the same day, grunt up the mountain a little slower the second time, and think the gnarly section sign would suit anywhere on the course. Foot placement is a many thousand time act of survival, mostly root and stub avoidance, with waist high grass sections and nature's assortment of rocks adding to the fun.

In the 85 degree heat of the road section, I thwart a voluminous deer fly welcome with a bandana hat cape trick, secured on the neck with my dark glasses croakies. This is an elemental summer trail run, and I'm loving it.

I finish the 50k in 8 hours 16 minutes, with about a quarter tank of energy left for tomorrow.

I'm in the cabin, spent and thinking, FUEL. I can't eat, so I take a nap. Forty minutes later, I've got an appetite. How many calories did I burn today and how many can I replace before tomorrow? Blueberry muffin for starters, then hard boiled eggs, spinach, carrots, tomato, avocado, cheese, peanuts, V-8, noodles, chocolate, volumes of water 'till I'm topped off – even now, I'm in caloric deficit vs. 24 hours ago.

Now comes the doubting period I often feel during an ultra event – is this too much, will I fail, will I quit? If I do, time and money spent for this two day running experience will have been squandered; worse, quitting would signal to me that I'm still the pretender I don't want to be. I lie down, fatigued, stuffed, and slide slowly into fitful sleep.

The start's at 8, and I'm up at 5. About 30 oz. of coffee, granola, an energy bar, then pack for self-serve aid stations – the marathon has three loops, so I can fuel up with potatoes and energy bars twice today. I've got the CamelBak loaded with Spiz again. Can't be more ready, and the mindset moves from iffy to "Can do."

We're down to six at the marathon, and I'm in fourth place after yesterday's 50k. Number 5 has a 14 minute lead on me from yesterday. I seldom think competitively in these events, but....

The course repeats yesterday's layout in the beginning, yet I still have to be careful at intersections. Two women take bonus miles together, for a three hour detour and will not finish today. There's more road than yesterday, but it's very rough - full of deep ruts, running water, and brush. Slow going again.

Roy tells us we'll go through an apple orchard; the apples are getting ripe, but the bears haven't gotten to them yet. I see fresh bear scat and feel the tingle of adrenalin shoot through me – puts more lift in the step.

Quality time is "mind of no mind," packed with focus on breathing cycles: the standard four step cycle; the two three step cycles (either two steps to inhale and one step to exhale, or one step to inhale and two steps to exhale); the two step breath cycle for climbing Crabbe Mtn.; and even a six step breath cycle for recovery to set a base of relaxation. Time flies in this.

Other time is "monkey brain" with random, outside thoughts trying to compete for attention – when will I finish, what's the time line, where are the other runners, why did I foolishly plop my foot in the water while crossing the beaver dam? Such involuntary distractions bring tension into the body. Time passes more slowly in monkey brain. Catching myself, I return the focus to running breath cycles, again and again.

Number 2 inbound to aid station;
number 5 outbound.

Coming up the mountain to complete the first loop, I see number 5 ahead of me. Two hours 35 minutes gone, and it looks like another 8 hour day. I fuel up and set out for lap two. Back into the woods and in a short while I see 5 coming toward me – one of us is going in the wrong direction. I say "Hey," and he says "Hey." And I say "OK?" and he looks at me funny. I say,

"Think you're going the wrong way," and he starts to cuss himself a blue streak, turning around to join me down the trail. I smell blood and take up the pace as fast as I can without danger of a fall. He stays with me briefly, then reels back. I really force it now to attempt a lasting separation from number 5. Still, knowing he lurks behind helps propel me forward more quickly.

On a good day near the end of a long event when I see about two hours remaining, I can really step it up, knowing there's no holding back of energy reserves – blast through to the end, you know. Today is such a day. For the first time ever, I think, "This so much fun, I don't want it to end."

Coming to the better road section, I know there's less than an hour and a half to go, and I find new power in my stride. At the last aid station, I soak the bandana and my head, telling the volunteer, "I am bleep'n GOOD TO GO." Then again in the last wet, boggy section the same thought rises - it's been a gnarly two days, but I'll miss them.

No kidding.

Out of the woods onto the ski slope, I power walk up the hill, managing even to run the last 200 yards up through to an 8 hour 9 minute marathon finish. I'm third in the CTC - with sympathy to 5, who fell to fourth on the day. I'm also the first American finisher.

How many Americans?

Hint: my cousin Tim once came back from a night on the town and proudly announced he and his date had just come in 3rd in a dance contest. "How many in the contest, Tim?" "Three," he replied.

———

Three weeks after Conquer the Canuck, I go to the Stowe Vt. Marathon for a last long run before Arkansas Traveller. I join my eldest daughter Chloe on Friday at the University of Vermont for a relaxing meal, driving east the next morning through low fog under a rising sun to the marathon start. Stowe is another shrine, like Woodstock, for all the times I've been there skiing at all ages and in all conditions: as a boy with my old family, and as a Dad with my new family. There's spirituality around Stowe, everywhere; it helps me run all the way up the monster hill past the Trapp Family ("Sound of Music") Lodge around mile 9 and makes energy out of my fumes in the final miles, to a hard (and slow) finish.

I am confident for Arkansas. I have read all the run reports, studied the course, established a pacing chart, and planned meticulously for every potential need in my drop bags. I failed at Laurel Highlands this year, just as I failed at Grasslands last year, but last year I rebounded to run 100 miles at Kettle Moraine. I will rebound again. Failure is just a motivator. I am standing at the end of the high board, not holding my daughter, but holding my other self, the failed one, and we are about to jump. Deedie wishes me good luck. I will not entertain negative thoughts.

———

ARKANSAS TRAVELLER 100 MILE TRAIL RUN
October 1-2, 2005

It's spelled with two l's because there's more to it than you'd think. While experts rate it an easier 100, AT is tougher than Vermont and Kettle Moraine. It's the rocks – rocky going on the ups, rocky going on the downs, rocky on the roads, rocky trails – just tell your loved ones you're going to a rock concert for the weekend.

Excellent aid stations help to offset the grind of the hard running surface. This combination makes AT doable for the lite 100 mile runner like me. Forget Hardrock, Wasatch, Bighorn, Massanutten, and the others made for uber mensch. If you want to bag a testy 100 miler that isn't a circular rope-a-dope layout, head down to Ouachita. RD's Chrissy and Stan will make sure you have every chance to put AT in your 100 mile bag for keeps.

The AT website has a nifty pace chart in two hour finishing increments for every aid station – put it in a pocket to keep track of your time. Expect eleven

AT goes out and back.

hours of darkness, and heat during the day. That's about all you need to know, and remember to bring your "A" game.

I set a realistic 28 hour goal using a combination of estimates I have refined over the years – take your percentage finishing rank from previous ultras and apply it to the past few years' AT times, take your past 100 mile times and apply a "toughness" quotient for AT, or follow the website guideline, and take seven times your marathon time for another look. By that last calculation I would finish half an hour past the 30 hour cut-off – which gives me something to think about before and during the event.

Along the way I think of *Chi Running*, Danny Dreyer's book: lean forward, let gravity and the psoas do the work while relaxing extremities – helpful. I also entertain the Buddhist philosophy of emptiness, which holds that there is no objective reality grounded in independent existence, and practice controlled breathing to calm the mind.

Running 100 miles is a purification rite. This is my first attempt without a pacer, to reach still deeper for refined pura vida. I remember the song, "Lonesome Highway." "You gotta walk that lonesome highway/ you gotta walk it by yourself/ 'cause nobody else can walk it for you/ you gotta walk it by yourself."

This I sing periodically after dark and into the next day, finding a good pacer in myself. I sing it to Mickey Rollins at his Smith Mountain aid station. Mickey prefers Bobby Bland, but he does acknowledge I have a point there, as far as my own deal is concerned.

I recall Joe Prusaitis' advice from Bighorn (a mountainous Wyoming 100 miler): "Never, never, ever give up," repeating this to myself especially in the 19 mile out and back from the Powerline aid station (miles 48.5 and 67.6) via the Turnaround (mile 58).

These supports fail to keep the bad angel away. Seeing that I am slipping from a 28 hour pace at the first Powerline to just under a 30 hour pace at Powerline the second time, he whispers, "You can drop here. They say you'll get a quick ride back, you can rest and sleep – probably can't beat 30 hours anyway – just not your day – maybe the end of your 100 mile career."

I'm about to quit. I discuss this with an aid station volunteer. He tells me to go for it - not only are the remaining 33 miles doable in 11 hours, but the last nine miles are downhill.

So?

So I swallow it. In this critical moment I exchange the physical for the mental, breaking through my own resistance. I resume running, just as he says I can. In my mind I push away from fear of failure, to embrace the fearful challenge. I press forward in near desperation, driven by adrenalin-loaded iron will. I will not stop, unless the clock stops me.

Alone in the dark I remember reading of Joe's 100 mile tendency to lie on his back and admire the stars. As much as I want to try this, I feel the press of time and stay erect. I chew eight pieces of Jolt caffeinated gum through the night to keep myself awake.

Different reports on AT include snakes and stinging bees. I see them both. More striking, though, is the sparkling reflection of spiders' eyes in my flashlight. At first I think these tiny reflecting lights on the ground are lost earrings. But as they keep appearing I examine more closely to see these lights belong to eight legged creatures out on patrol. They can see at night, in contrast to us humans, who need lanterns. Who's better equipped?

On a height scale comparison, 100 miles to a spider extends just beyond the reach of my stronger flashlight. To think they will never in their lifetime wander far from where I see them – and how many tonight are being crushed under runners' feet? I can almost hear them screaming. Not one other runner seems to know this is going on – so much for objective reality. What's happening around me doesn't matter. I'm driven like the spiders in survival mind – anything less than completion will mean spiritual death. At Winona (mile 84) my watch tells me I've got a 32 minute cushion on 30 hours. I begin to believe that I can make it.

RD Chrissy Ferguson (center) at Chicken Gap, mile 69.7. Chrissy runs the 100 miler, too.

AT aid stations have plentiful ice – cold drink is a huge positive. There's chicken noodle soup – very useful in the later miles. Aid station volunteers emerge from nowhere with your drop bag to attend needs as if you were a brother – that's how they feel about it. What a difference they make. Heck, one of them even pulled me away from the bad angel – I owe him this enduring energy. Essential people.

Coming back over Rocky Gap (mile 87), the rock rubble beyond comprehension triggers in me a question, "Has anyone ever counted all the rocks in

Rocky Gap?" To this the aid station volunteer just smiles sympathetically.

Real and unreal mix freely. "Hey," I say to another runner, "we went by this place this morning." "Yes," he replies, "except it was yesterday morning." Four miles to the next aid station. Sunlight. I feel energy. Shapes in the woods trick me into thinking they are the next aid station. They are not. Even knowing this, I keep thinking they are. We see what we want to see. I am so happy.

In the Buddhist cosmos I am moving from the desire realm, characterized by feeling and pain, to the form realm, free from any experience of pain, permeated with bliss. Says the Dalai Lama, beings in this realm possess bodies composed of light.

I feel nothing but the sun's rays on my head and back. I am light; I am finishing.

The AT's last gift comes when I meet up with Mike Stansberry and his 19 year old daughter pacing him. My daughter Lila paced me at Kettle last year, so now the three of us have much to talk about, as we slow to a walk. We toy with a sub 29 hour assault on the finish, but agree to enjoy the last few miles reflecting on family and our ultrarunning experiences. It all comes back together for me then.

Suddenly we see the finish banner, tumble down the last 100 yards with fanfare, music, and Chrissy's warm greeting, to completion.

Oh, what a feeling….

Author finishing Arkansas Traveller

Did I mention the 100 Mile Run Arkansas Traveller license plate frame we got in our goody bag? It wouldn't be right to put that thing on your car unless you actually finished the darn race. Gotta say, mine looks pretty good right now.

Thanks and gratitude to Chrissy, Stan, and the crew.

———

CHAPTER SIX – RUNNING ON EMPTY

I remember being struck, when I was just a beginner, by how many different kinds of people run marathons and ultramarathons. I found that ultramarathoners have a more relaxed way about them, a steadier gaze. I think I am more that way now, too, after about fifty marathons and ultras. There are people who run with "IN MEMORY OF --------" stenciled on their backs to salve their grief; and there are people who really ARE running away from something in their lives that is so uncomfortable they can't sit still with it. I've seen too-proud former ultramarathon champions - still fit - who no longer enter events because they can't stand not being able to win anymore. There are rookies who don't know how to finish and old veterans who don't know how to quit – both kinds usually meet with injury. There are many people who run long distance because they are confused, hoping that when they finish, whatever it is will be clearer to them. It often isn't, but they hold hope. And there are many, many ultrarunners who keep going simply because running makes them happy. These ones have learned to accept who they are and who they are becoming. Thought selection and mind control were not theirs when they began their journey; it accrued to them gradually, over many months and years of strenuous, solitary time alone, in which they got to know themselves truthfully. Truth is hard to know and harder to accept, but living true is the only way to happiness. This I believe.

INTERLUDE

We are going on a year end family vacation – New Year's in the Bahamas! Chloe will graduate from college in May, and this will be our last chance to be together in a vacation setting before she becomes an honest working woman next summer. Before Chloe and Lila come home for the trip, Deedie takes Maggie and me to Cambridge for Christmas carols:

96TH ANNUAL CHRISTMAS CAROLS – MEMORIAL CHURCH

HARVARD SQUARE – THE HARVARD UNIVERSITY CHOIR

On a Sunday afternoon we attend this very popular event, begun in 1910. In the music notes, we read: "Towards the end of the service the congregation is invited to participate in the singing of "Silent Night" in English or in German. This practice memorializes that most moving episode during World War One when, on Christmas Day in 1914, soldiers from both sides of the trenches laid down their arms and climbed into no-man's land to sing this carol."

We sing in Latin, "Adeste Fideles" ("O Come All Ye Faithful"), followed by a reading from an odd sounding pastor whom Maggie describes later as "Strange - I don't like that man."

The choir sings "Ave Virgo Sanctissima," then the congregation sings "Lo How a Rose E'er Blooming," then the choir, "Ave Maria." My favorite phrase here: "ora pro nobis peccatoribus nunc et in hora mortis nostrae" ("pray for us sinners now and at the hour of our death").

Then another smooth reading, from an assisting minister, displaying substantial caloric excess and a too-tight collar, presumably gotten in seminary days.

Choir: "Puer Natus in Bethlehem" - Latin with a neat German refrain: "singet, jubiliret, triumphiret, unserm herren dem konig der ehren."

Congregation: "Personent Hodie" sung in Latin, composed in Germany, 1350.

Choir: two more carols, one in lively Spanish.

Odd sounding pastor, again reading on the three wise men, and pronouncing "myrrh" - "meeurrdre" – kind of like squeezing pus out of a zit. Nice one, pastor.

Choir, then congregation, then choir, to "O Magnum Mysterium." I think of ancient rulers forcing Christianity on the masses to keep them psychically sedated, of the myth of Jesus being a good message oft wrought bad - crusades, etc. And I think of my own forced religious upbringing – HAD to buy in – and subsequent withdrawal from "faith," as they call it. Would "entrapment" be a better description?

This religion is theirs, not mine. I have my own version now – but the pomp, the circumstance, the gear, the ages, the soldiers in the trenches dropping their guns to sing in different languages – God (!) – the power of it all is so humbling.

A lumpy man to my right lips the Latin songs but does not sing in English. Now comes "Silent Night," and I whisper to Maggie on my left, "German or English (we hold programs with both versions)?" She: "Who's going to sing it in German?" Me: "I will, and maybe the man to my right will, too."

Then – wonder – the lumpy man begins "Stille Nacht! Heilige Nachte!" in a voice so plaintive, so longing, so eager, that he begins the next line several beats ahead of the music – me singing in German with him, and three heads to the left I see Lila's former 10th grade English teacher, also choosing the German... it's the Epiphany revisited!

This moment stirs wild thoughts of warriors emerging from trenches in 1914; ninety-five previous congregations standing here singing; Germans in 1350 quilling Latin hymns – my 15 year old daughter's pure voice lilting, "Son of God, love's pure light."

And finally "Hark ! The Herald Angels Sing" with "light and life to all He brings/ risen with healing in His wings/ born that we no more may die/ born to raise us from the earth/ born to give us second birth."

We leave exhilarated. It's all so vast, and I'm so very small, so glad to be Christian on this day. God just won't go away. I cannot deny it.

Buddhist thinkers describe "original mind" as the developed mental state in which extraneous ideas – even random thoughts – can be turned away, as the result of meditative practices. Parentally imposed judgments, apocryphal truths set by teachers, coaches, friends, politicians, gurus, religious imperatives, the whole wad of stuff that tells us what to think, or even how to think, can be purged, so that a person is able to experience original thinking: one's very own thoughts and ideas. What we've been told is superego overlay, contrary to the simpler way, in which the mind is not held captive by outside prejudice. That stuff is the glue holding id and ego also. It's all just clutter that burdens and limits a perfectly good, original mind.

———

JANUARY 6, 2006 – THE BAHAMAS

Words fail me. The urge to dip completely underwater puts me frog stroking along the clean sandy bottom. I will go this way until I reach Africa, or if my breath fails, until I am a changed person. I want to lose something. After almost six decades, I know what it is. It's the mask, the pretension.

For many years I've had this recurring dream: I'm in a large school building; teachers, the authority, keep me there. I can't get out of the building. Then last night, I dream a different dream: I set a large building on fire, floor by floor. School children are in it, asking me what I am doing. They do not suffer. We all get out.

Man made religion a comfort food for the mind. The mask also. People cannot see themselves. The woman with red lipstick painted beyond her lips, the man wearing pants tight in the crotch. We find it uncomfortable being who we are. There's something missing. We try to cover up what's not there, yet others see that we have not. We don't know this. The pretension.

Neither do I seek to be a teacher. Just clear of it all. The presence comes from within, from a place not seen but felt. People take comfort behind the mask. It becomes a permanent fixture. I am the mask. I am not myself. That's too scary.

My breath fails me. I surface. My wife and three daughters present smiles and expressions of surprise. What do they see?

———

MORNING HOME RUN WITH DOG

Dark. Full yellow moon looks through the window, drawing me out. Morning stretch and dog on hill clear low moon view; a shooting star, quick but certain. Big Dipper straight up. Warm air flows up into my lungs deeply, closed eyes like the swim exhaling I open, seeing, being. Orgasmic fleeting sensory wonder; earth mother me so tiny standing there dog watching.

———

AVALON 50 MILE RUN
January 14, 2006

(see also Chapter One; page 14)

About five miles after the start, dawn's light frames a runner ahead of me, slow-loping up the steep hill to Catalina's ridgeline. I press to pass, but soon she passes me, holding to her slow lope, while I walk. I think, "Here's a steady pace that suits me – I'll try to stay with her." Along the ridgeline, I draw alongside; we chat. Christine tells me she's from Sacramento; I tell her I'm from Boston. She has a tight hamstring, says it's slowing her down. I pull ahead on a downhill. At the Little Harbor aid station (mile 17), as I reload my CamelBak and change socks, she arrives and quickly gets through the transition, just ahead of me.

At the dog track, Christine would be "Swifty," and I would be the chasing greyhound. She may or may not know I'm pulled by her pace, and that if I were not, I'd be slower. I draw past again, saying, "Hi, Sacramento," and she, "Hi, Boston." The stretch to the Two Harbors (mile 24) turnaround has a long uphill which I run, because I know Christine is chasing me (she may or may not be chasing, but I imagine that she is). Heading back, I see her; crossing, we say "Hi Boston" and "Hi Sacramento" again – a soft gesture of friendship in a hard effort of running. On the return to Little Harbor I try to repeat the fast pace I found in this stretch five years ago, but this time, mud cakes on the shoes, for much slower going. I get anxious that Sacramento might be closing on me, but think her shoes by now have mud cakes like mine. I still press.

Transitioning through Little Harbor (mile 32) again, now with fresh shoes, I begin the long, irregular thirteen mile climb to the ridgeline. Three hours later, I pass through the point of departure, becoming lighter and more tunneled, stroking methodically. To my right, Sacramento draws even and slowly moves ahead. I'm fully extended at my pace and cannot chase to close on her. She lengthens the distance between us and disappears over a hilltop. I plod on, thankful that I have been able to draw on her energy thus far.

In the final crazy downhill miles to the finish, I imagine that I might catch her somehow; greyhounds think that of Swifty, too. Finally, sprinting the last 200 yards to the finish, I see her walking away, finishing medal in hand. I'm extremely tunneled, but I hear her shout, "Go, Boston!"

I finish, grinning.

———

IRON HORSE 100K – JACKSONVILLE, FLORIDA
March 4, 2006

"Where are you going?"

"Going to vanish."

"Is that a place?"

"Can't say – never been there."

Somewhere near mile 54, my left leg buckles. I've been looking for a trigger – is this it?

I pick the inaugural Iron Horse 100k run for its layout: double out and back 15.5 mile sections on a flat-paved-straight rail bed, free of obstructions. More often I prefer trail ultras for their scenery and softer ground cushion. This time out I want a singular opportunity to enter into "no mind" as easily as possible: focus on a spot 10 feet ahead and dive into the deep end.

It's not that easy, I find. No short cuts. Patience is one of the many things I lack. Then again, there's plenty of entertainment today: fourteen and a half hours of it.

I learn in three minutes that race director Chris Rodatz has reconstructed his approach to life. I will find out why later. We stand ready, from the 6 a.m. start time until 6:03. Still dark, still the same 30 odd runners ready to go.

Still.

Chris waits for everything to settle, for stragglers to join in, for the quiet moment to come, then to pray: "May god on this day hold you in the palm of his hand." For all of this, right here and right now, Chris is thankful, beyond our understanding.

Thus fortified, we set off in morning darkness.

"No mind" is where I want to go because so much of thinking is conditioned, not original. Why walk in someone else's footprints? After running for eight hours or more, my physiological hold on mind activity loosens, allowing me to not think. The experience "to not think" arrives after much conditioning, many long runs, beginning with "thinking to not think." That's almost it, but not it. To not think is the gateway to original thinking.

It's the fullness of self-discovery. It's putting your experience into a memory bank where no foreign deposits reside. Foreign deposits like "spooky things jump out in the dark," or "barking dogs are dangerous," or most conventional takes on what makes success or happiness. Well-intentioned parents, authority figures, or friends put such foreign deposits in our memory banks: "Always try to be the best," or "Learn to accept failure." Intuitively, we don't distinguish between our own deposits and those placed by others, but they are worlds apart. Even in common sense and intuition, what we might take for original thinking is so often cluttered with ideas and learned responses we did not ourselves create. Do you like to use another person's toothbrush?

No mind, original thought. The room in my brain is a musty attic loaded with stuff beyond its usefulness that hasn't yet been thrown out. "See this picture? That's me when I was…." Out with it!

Settling, I pace at 12 minutes per mile. The business of running ultramarathons with competence to finish manufactures the product of original thinking. I'm slow, but I know the last finisher is the slowest winner.

Says Yiannis Kouros, this world's most accomplished ultrarunner, "During the ultras I come to a point where my body is almost dead. My mind has to take leadership. When it is very hard there is a war going on between the body and the mind. If my body wins, I will have to give up; if my mind wins, I will continue. At that time I feel that I stay outside of my body. It is as if I see my body in front of me; my mind commands and my body follows. This is a very special feeling, which I like very much…It is a very beautiful feeling and the only time I experience my personality separate from my body, as two different things."

(Yiannis Kouros interview, UltraRunning Magazine, March 1990)

Every half mile there's a painted number in the middle of the path, indicating how many miles you are from one end or the other. Chris has set out four aid stations – two at either end, and two roughly equidistant from either end, about five miles apart. So I find food and drink I don't have to carry with me about once every hour. If I were Yiannis, aid would be more like every half hour. In the end, the theoretical Yiannis and I will have used about the same amount of energy: mine slower burning, his faster burning. My fire peat, his fire tungsten.

If a runner paces faster than his competence, he will have to give up, because his body fails. Runners knowing their competence through many trials can rate themselves as they go along. I'm stroking away, cap protecting from the sun, eyes fixed on the spot, my shadow cast in front of me as I go out westerly to the turnaround.

I think, "If I were very good at no mind, at not thinking, I probably would not have to follow my shadow." The shadow persists in leading me.

It's just over three hours to the 15.5 mile turnaround.

And again just over three hours to the 31 mile halfway start/finish. In this second lap of four, I press in the last 10 miles, running slightly up tempo at 11 ½ minute miles to reach the time objective I'd decided on in the days leading up to this event. That number comes from how well training has gone, and a lot of hunch.

Half-way, I change into newer shoes that will be kinder to the feet later on and gulp orzo in chicken broth I've kept in my drop bag for fuel. Out in 6 hours 28 minutes.

Right away in the third lap, I feel low energy – it's the solid food, and maybe from not being fully recovered from the Avalon 50 miler seven weeks ago. The next few miles go disturbingly slower. I've squandered at least 8 minutes versus plan in just the last three miles – and there are 28 miles left to go. OK, think - try this: just go along at a comfortable pace and use the mile markers to see what this pace is – 15 minute miles. I can't believe this! I can WALK 15 minute miles. Another mile, then another: both 15 minutes. Dumbfounded, I think, "Shoot, maybe if I just walk, the pace would be the same." I time the next ½ mile and see it's a 16 minute mile walking pace. I can't afford to spend an additional 25 minutes in choosing the walking strategy. Back to running.

Chris has set a generous 15 hour cut off for this 62.2 mile event, and I figure that if I don't make 15 minute miles through to the end, I'll risk getting the dreaded hook – Did Not Finish. DNF is the product of non-original thinking. OK, new plan here: it's going to be 15 minute miles for the rest of the way. Allowing not more than 5 minutes at the 46.7 mile turnaround to add ice to my CamelBak, I can finish in under 15 hours.

At times I cannot run, and so walk until I can start up again. Must start up. Must. I complete the third lap in four hours, leaving 4 ½ hours to complete the fourth lap within the cut off. Here comes Chris alongside on his bicycle, deep voice giving soft encouragement, father-like: "C'mon, Mike, keep it moving." I am the same age, yet I listen as would a son. I start up again, and from mile 48 to the end I keep running. Ancient philosophers say objective reality for us exists only in relation to others – alone we cannot experience it. Alone, I might have just walked.

Now after six o'clock, and 10 miles to go, I figure at this pace I will finish at 8:33 p.m., or in 14 hours and 30 minutes. Must. Stroke.

Then dusk. I know I will soon be enveloped in darkness. This is OK – I train in morning darkness regularly with no flashlight. Here too, I have no flashlight. I tell myself, this is now just another 10 mile training run, like so many hundreds of others.

The leg buckles. I stumble, catch, and start up again. The effect is a slap in the face. This is the moment of departure. Dark, silent path, alone, pupils open like saucers, releasing all convention. I have lost my mind. I observe myself running from another place, an outside place. An essential place.

With no mind, I know that spooky things can only jump out in the dark if I let them, and I will not. Not thinking, I know that barking dogs are not dangerous, just barking dogs. I am whole, I am empty, I am running toward 8:33 p.m. Only that.

Now the moon points a finger at me. There on the ground is my night shadow, going easterly. I am the moon's whimsy, nothing else. Now going very well.

Four miles or one hour left and approaching neighborhoods, I think, why not let a spooky thing jump out, just for fun? And so shadows become monsters, and I read tomorrow's local news: "Runner Mauled By Alligator On Bike Path." For a moment I feel real fear before willing it away.

To my left at 300 yards from the spot-lit house I see a person letting dogs out. Startled barks, then a charge towards me – mean aggressive dog sounds fill the night. There's a tight fence between us, yet I feel adrenalin's fire hose pressure race through me, instinctive fear of survival. Safe, I enjoy this psycho-physiological rush from so deep it precedes even original thought.

In the last two and one-half miles I'm back together, cruising to the finish. On a little rise in the last 200 yards, there stands Chris. As I cross the line from one world to the next he says my time is 14 hours and 31 minutes. 8:34 p.m. - I have missed my final estimate by one minute.

Chris joins me in the darkness to chat. He tells me he's running ultras a little slower now, after having part of his lung removed. I tell him about my ultra quest, my learning process. His story is much the same. Our best times are behind us now, but we would not trade this time for anything. We can see more clearly now, for all that we have done; in this we are brothers.

An hour later, I'm in The Waffle House across from the motel, ordering eggs, potatoes, and lots of orange juice. Women working there wearing "Daytona Bike Week 2006" Harley vests don't even raise an eyebrow when I quietly ask for more water, saying, "I'm dehydrated, just ran 62 miles." They're thinking, "Imagine, it's early on Saturday night and already people are telling stories."

———

ANOTHER YEAR, ANOTHER PLAN ALTERED

I wanted 2006 to be the victory lap year. I planned to return to event venues I'd visited in past years, the ones I like the most: Catalina Island, Bull Run, Vermont 100. Up until this year I've made a point of going to different running events. There are so many beautiful places to visit and new faces to see. I went a second time to Miwok only to redeem my first attempt DNF there. After finishing my third 100 at Arkansas, I developed a distinct awareness that the passing of time would limit my future options. Iron Horse is nearly the same layout as Withlacoochee, but it took me two hours longer. Four years apart; three per cent slower every year roughly makes up the two hour difference. How many more 100 mile events can I finish under the typical 30 hour cut-off?

So I return to Manassas in early April for the Bull Run event, especially enjoying the camaraderie of Friday night's pasta feed. Run day Saturday badly surprises the weatherman and the runners, with more rain and cold temperature than anyone expects. Under-clothed and feeling hypothermic, I gut it out until reflecting for about two nanoseconds on Scott Mills' question, "Are you having fun?" Answering silently with a definite "NO," I pull out after 28 miles.

2006 Bull Run: wet and cold.

In attempting to rebound from Bull Run, in late April I enter the inaugural 24-Hour Adventure Trail Run in Triangle, Virginia. I hope to make it a 13 to 15 hour, 49 or 56 mile (seven mile loops) training run for Vermont. I bomb there, too, from oppressive heat and a general lack of motivation.

I'm having serious difficulty rising to the hard training and steely determination I need to take to any ultra, in order to have a good outing. Maybe my true self is whispering to me that it still remains distant. I've largely discarded the wear of extraneous thought structures, but am still not comfortably fitted into Buddha mind.

I'm looking for an easy way, and there is none. To this point, I have run three 100 mile events in three consecutive years. For each of them, I've trained using the regimen that I proved could work for me, but this year I'm trying something different. Instead of 10 mile or longer runs during weekdays, with alternating days off, and long single or back-to-back runs on weekends, I'm running every day; shorter outings with less total weekly mileage than during prior training cycles. It's an experiment in self-indulgence. I imagine that I can run long events without applying the proven method. I'm posing as a wily veteran, now capable since I've been there before and I know how to execute. The truth is I'm fatigued just thinking about those long hard training runs. I don't have the commitment to do them. I think I possess some cumulative wherewithal, but in truth I'm pretending again. Rationalizing this avoidance is a long way from Buddha mind. I realize that if I don't take myself to the next level of commitment, it certainly will not come to me. I've done this before; done it in my life with people, too. Half-way measures get half-assed results.

Time before Vermont is running short. I decide to regroup simply and locally, hoping to renew the proven training regimen. Returning to the Nipmuck

Trail Marathon could be just the ticket to put body and mind into proper form for the Vermont 100.

———

CHAPTER SEVEN: HEADING HOME

NIPMUCK TRAIL MARATHON - "NUTS"

May 28, 2006

On finishing the Nipmuck trail marathon the first time, in 2001, I said, "Leave that one to the masochists."

I went back; maybe I'm nuts. Maybe all 114 men, together with the 28 women who finished it this year, are nuts, too. There's something contagious about it.

The first time I ran Nipmuck, it tripped me down nine times – I counted them. Skinned palms, elbows, and knees; nice dirt and mud in the cuts, and poison ivy as an itchy keepsake for weeks to come.

Why do it – why do it again?

Rich Busa is 76, a stud running legend. We're chatting before the start, and I compliment Rich on winning the national 10k snowshoe championship at Bolton Valley this year. He tells me he also won the previous year in Anchorage, but was alone in his age group. An up front guy, Rich – gotta respect that.

This gets me thinking, "Next year I'll be in the sixty plus age group; I could start winning some iron." Just last year I was the first American finisher at the New Brunswick, Canada "Conquer the Canuck" trail runs (only one American contestant).

Some people never get tired of wanting to finish first.

Race Director Dave Raczkowski puts on his pre-race briefing, which is really a stand-up trail runner comedy skit. Odd, but the crowd gets it. We begin nearly twenty minutes after the official start time, no big deal. The funnel effect of 160+ runners into single file on the Nipmuck trail makes for some early walking – it's a good way to warm into it. Everybody understands there will be no marathon PR's here.

The course starts 6+ miles out, then back. Sections of the trail are familiar to me, even after five years. It seems like a reunion with a long lost friend. Twenty minutes from the turnaround, I meet the lead group of four runners - tight, fast, surging up the hill. Most trail runners don't run up hills, they walk. Further down, the path slopes toward the Fenton River, its muddy banks trying to pull you in. Runners slow down here to grab hold of something, like walking through a subway car in motion.

My first CamelBak is loaded with Spiz, a highly digestible, caloric mix of nutrition that's my early stage staple. I hurry and sip, sip and hurry. In planning strategy, I figure Nipmuck might take me 6 ½ hours, the second out and back section maybe an hour longer than the first.

Around mile ten, I come up behind Rich, who's motoring efficiently, with quick feet among the rocks and snags – 76! There's a road crossing. Legging over the guard rail, I rush to pass him and another companion runner. In a slippery climb through the next uphill section, I try to put some distance between us.

Back into the start/finish area, I switch CamelBaks, the new one loaded with Ultragen, an energy boosting recovery drink, taking half a peeled orange and a hand held water bottle with ginseng tea in it – this next out and back will be hotter. I've become much quicker in transitions like this – couldn't have been more than three minutes.

Five minutes into the second out and back, I see Rich ahead of me again – must have gone straight through the start/finish when I was changing gear. As I close behind him, he sees me and tosses a cordial greeting. We chat, high stepping down the rocky trail. I'm feeling good right now, but it comes to me that it's all I can do to keep up with a guy seventeen years older – either he's in great shape (yes) or I'm getting slower (yes). Something deep down tells me I cannot allow him to finish ahead of me. This is when the 2006 edition of the Nipmuck becomes a contest between Rich and Mike. Or is it really between Mike and Mike?

We approach a stream crossing, where Dave Raz has put a plastic bucket on a string at the water's edge for a quick cooling douse, if you like. Rich likes, and I see my chance, jetting past him as he splashes cool water on his warm head.

My head's warm too, but there's work to be done. Next comes a half-mile road section, descending. I put the hammer down here. Now's my chance to establish separation.

So 15 miles into it, I switch from hunter to hunted. New energy envelops me from the pervading motivator – flight. In this state of mind you don't want to look back because if the pursuer is closing, seeing him will break you. Better to press forward with all you've got – more likely to discourage the hunter, who will think you confident.

The lead runners are passing by now; they will finish two and a half hours ahead of me. No doubt they are immersed in their own mental games. I did not purposely choose this test of pursuer/pursued, but it's very real and it's forcing a hard pace. Where I normally would walk, I speed walk, and where I normally would lope, I run, driven, driven.

Down a set of steep wooden stairs to the second turnaround at mile 19.4, I splash water on my head at the aid station and wheel back for the last quarter. Soon after I'm back on the trail, climbing, Rich passes by – I figure maybe five minutes back.

I still feel pursued, but I also sense a clear advantage. Gradually my chemistry shifts from flight-driven to a calmer, more self-contained recognition of purpose, time and place: I'm hot and tired, my will still pressing to run when my body wants to walk, knowing now I have just a few miles to the finish. It's a matter of closing strong, wringing the last energy reserves from a deep place that I don't visit otherwise in ordinary life, measuring my position against the original time objective. When I cross the stream with the water bucket, indulgently I douse my head – from here I figure a sub 6 ½ hour finish is doable.

All along I saved the memory of having lost it here last time: In 2001, I bonked badly near the end and had to death-march to the finish. This time I've been pushing water down all day, taking electrolytes and conserving sufficient energy to be ready to attack the final section.

With a mile and a half to go, I pass two contestants now walking – they cheer me on: "Great finish, guy, keep it up!" I was in their shoes five years ago, and I hope they'll be in mine the next time. Trail runners are a mutual encouragement society – most people passing each other exchange a "Good job" or a "Way to go," no matter their advantage or relative pace. We might be nuts, but we unfailingly support each other – it comes from the shared experience of hard work.

And so through to a 6:12 finish, better than I thought I could do. Those few minutes I captured I owe mostly to Rich and to the spontaneous fear/flight incentive that was discomforting yet productive. Stripped to shorts, I pour a gallon jug of water over myself to get some of the grit off. A fellow nearby says, "This is my first time. That was MUCH harder than I expected it to be."

I recall five years ago, on the second out and back, hearing one runner say to his companion, "If you FEEL like throwing up, then THROW UP!" This pretty much sums up what to expect at the Nipmuck trail marathon.

During my daughter Chloe's college graduation ceremony a week ago, one of the honored student speakers told attentive listeners that she threw up

Nipmuck trail running – if you don't look down, you'll go down.

BEFORE giving her address. Maybe that could be an effective strategy to get ready for next year's Nipmuck. Think I'll run that one by Dave Raz – he'll probably know.

Or he might just shrug his shoulders and say, "NUTS ! "

THEN AND NOW

My most intense sports adrenalin moments came right before football games, in the tunnel that leads into the Yale Bowl – the clack of cleats on concrete echoed a primitive rhythm that prodded the entire team into wild potential energy about to turn explosively kinetic. I waited for that peaking moment, imagining its surge would carry me beyond the boundaries of my warrior uniform to find extraordinary powers of speed and strength, exceeding even my well tuned physical abilities.

Before a typical ultramarathon, people wait in early morning darkness or pre-dawn light, for the race director to say, "Go," in the manner one would tell a pet to venture outside to do its business. There's a calm. I imagine a painter holding his palette, contemplating an untouched canvas, his mind now prepared to guide him into a flow of creativity. The ultrarunner's day is that canvas, his physical self the brush, his mind and spirit the artist standing there about to apply expressions that live in his imagination. They took shape in the weeks leading up to that moment of calm before the start, where in training runs, the athlete worked an image of every aspect of his approaching performance; from footwear and gear, to nutrition, to the appropriate pace. The artist runner understands to work his physical self into a fluidity that leads to unconscious equilibrium. His feet strike the ground with the force of feathers. From the point of departure hours after the start, pure expression comes alive. In slow twitch expression, the athlete applies his art thoughtfully, carefully, lovingly.

———

VERMONT 100
July 15, 2006

I set my tent in the field with about one hundred others planning to run the next morning. It's over 90 degrees and humid. There's water and mud everywhere, more than people usually see here, even in springtime.

I listen to voices of experience say, "Go out faster in the cool morning, slow down in the hot part of the day. Take a lot of electrolytes and water and wait to pick up the pace toward nighttime when it cools off a little." I try that but shoot my wad early and never recover. I rest nearly half an hour at Camp Ten Bear (mile 46) before going on, nearer the cut off times than I'd like to be. Agony Hill this time runs with mud so bad I don't even notice the mosquitoes. When I get beyond the top to the next aid station, I tell them, "Stick a fork in me, I'm done." It's 6:30, and I've been going fourteen and a half hours. I cannot bear the thought of attempting still another fifty miles to the finish. I am discouraged.

I wanted Vermont to be the capstone of my victory lap year. Instead, I fail here, just as I failed at Bull Run;

one too hot, one too cold. Victory "lapse" is more like it. My friend Vicky asks me why I dropped. Without hesitation, I answer, "Insufficient training and lack of motivation."

———

The hardest days come after a DNF, and I've had three of them already this year. My ambition was to make a fourth consecutive 100 mile finish at Vermont. The other DNF's I see as training runs and don't cut so deep. After my first 100, I thought that running one 100 miler every year would both test my ability and satisfy my abiding interest in the spiritual rewards that come from the experience; these would be my once a year, 100 mile pilgrimages. Now I face being left behind in my own movie. I've got too little, and it's too late.

I have put myself in another trap. I begin to understand that in my fascination with the spiritual aspects of ultrarunning, I persist in the delusion that if I carry the idea of emptiness to the starting line, it will offset ill-preparedness from lack of hard physical training. Avalon allowed me access to emptiness only because I was well conditioned going into it. Iron Horse gave an indifferent result because I put emptiness in front of conditioning. Vermont was a bomb because I banked on emptiness much too heavily. Emptiness laughed at me as I labored up

Agony Hill, spent down to my last penny. "Who's empty now?" it mocked.

When I started going long, I felt pride when my friends would say, "There goes Mike; he runs ultramarathons, even 100 milers." As ultrarunning brought me closer to my true self, I realized this was not how I wanted to be recognized, at all. I'm not running to impress; I'm running for joy. My friends frame a two-dimensional picture, the same one I'm trying to extinguish, defined by accomplishment. In sustaining the myth of a person identified by accomplishment, my friends do not succeed at being my friends. I do not judge them; I just smile with them. They are still my friends. Finishing 100 miles is one part accomplishment and ninety-nine parts spiritual enrichment. I am told that enlightened people do not bring attention to themselves by saying, "Look! Look at all my spiritual richness!" I am told they are content in anonymity and silence: "Who knows, doesn't tell; who tells, doesn't know." My weakness is that I keep seeking attention, while pretending to deny it.

Looking out from this trap, I'm the guy mesmerized by the wonder of himself, like Proust in the cork-lined room, writing remembrances. I am presumptuous; I have taken myself too seriously. I thought I was onto something, but instead, that something has put a bag over my head. Fucking ego!

———

MOUNT TOBY 14 MILER
August 27, 2006

(see also Chapter One, page 5)

Ruch Busa, my hero

I have to keep going. People lose their way all the time. It's not so important that one gets lost; it's getting found again that matters. I'm here at the start of the annual Mount Toby 14 miler, a 1900 foot up and down trail run. I hear the echo of Scott Mills' question, "Are you having fun?" from Bull Run. Today, I'm out for fun, nothing more.

Here comes Rich Busa, my hero. As always, I congratulate him for being the person he is – the oldest one and still running like a deer. I first met Rich on the Friday before the Vermont 100 three years ago. We had lunch together, then met again by chance Sunday morning around 1:30 in mile 82; he finished soon after I did. Rich tells me he often wins his age group in events because there aren't any others his age, but that will change; when people like me get older we'll surely have more company, because people know how to take care of themselves better now. I'm elated to hear the news. I hope all of us never stop running.

———

SERENDIPITOUS THREE

ONE

I'm lying in the dark tent, cold. Mid-September days in southern New Hampshire stay warm, but nights are cool. I forgot that – my sleeping bag's at home. I'm wrapped in thin sheets, a single blanket, and all the clothes I brought, peering at my watch to see if it's not too crazy to get up.

Owls begin their echoing rounds– one distant off my right shoulder, then a companion, more distant, behind my head. Owl time. I put on the headlamp, unzip, and light a match in the pine needle tinder: fire. Boil water on the propane burner: coffee.

I sit in a low-slung chair; socked feet up close to the flames, hold the hot cup in both hands, and take a first sip. Looking up, I see dark blue, a star-filled, infinite canopy – there's the universe, and here's me, by a warming fire.

Pre-dawn. A jay starts calling, urged with indiscriminate sweepings of testosterone: "Give me attention; give me love!" Males often don't choose more subtle approaches. In the trees, something's moving; a squirrel cruising for acorns sends them down in discreet thumps. I sit still, quiet, sensing.

As I drive out from the campsite, directly into the low rising sun, my first spoken words bubble out: "Good day for a run." I hear this as if spoken by a companion. Cutting through low fog, I pause as eighteen wild turkeys cross the road. Minds in nature.

The Mount Pisgah 50k trail run – single track, woodsy, early fall colors. It's chilly at the start. I see the lean muscled bare torso and knotted legs of Craig Wilson, Hardrock veteran. I'm weak by comparison, but it's my body that I carry, no one else's. The trail and the process are familiar – I've done this before – work into a comfortable rhythm, back of the pack, allow stored energy to come alive, think of nothing but here and now.

When I reach the third of five aid stations at mile 17, I see that this pace would take me to the finish

close to my time three years ago – that's my goal.
The volunteers remind me of the big hill in the next
section, over the top of Mt. Pisgah. Working up the
slope, I know my now slower pace puts me behind,
but this is no surprise – stay calm, stay focused,
press it.

Then down, joining the five mile loop – I see a runner
ahead of me, already six miles forward, completing
the loop I have not yet started. Could I ever have
been so fast? No matter; I'm just pressing it –only
that matters.

At the end of the pond I pass another pilgrim – he
catches my energy, following close behind. This urges
me on: I will not be passed. His hard breathing puts
me into more concentrated focus; once or twice I
think he will catch me, but he must be struggling,
too, as I keep a slim lead. We're working together, an
unspoken pact to create still more performance. I
know he wants it; he's challenging me to want it more.

I come to a parking lot. Two walkers seem startled,
saying, "Are you in a race? Look, he has a number."
I'm so spent that I'm walking, too ("Where's my
pursuer? Catching me?") and make the joke: "Does
it look like I'm in a race, walking like this?" I know
in my mind to use everything to motivate: "They're
wondering if I might run, he's closing. I've got to
get moving."

The final woods section has two bear hill climbs. I
don't remember their being so tough – then out onto

the road for a final mile, full bore, saving nothing. One last darn hill, then done.

Minutes later, my pursuer comes through. I wait for him to recover enough to accept my thanks for pushing me. He replies: "I tried to catch you, but I couldn't." – in this way thanking me in return. So it goes.

If it's true that people on average get three percent slower every year, comparing my finish time to the last one, I see that I'm just an average guy. Broke seven hours, anyway.

TWO

I'm doing back-to-back 20 milers on a weekend, now in the second 10 of the out and back on Sunday. A runner named Zsuzsanna joins me at the beginning of the famous Boston Marathon hills, ending with Heartbreak. She's on a long training run, too, for the New York Marathon. We speak the same runner's language, she with a thick Hungarian accent. She stops to pay homage to the Johnny Kelley bronze – even knows about some of the ultras I've run – refreshingly candid, too. I've quickened my pace to keep up with her. I always "sprint" up Heartbreak, and today's no different. As I pull away from Zsuzsanna with deep heavy hard breathing, a wondrous energy envelops me – the same I felt for the first time, I think, several weeks ago at the Mt. Toby event – uber mensch stuff. She glides up to catch me at the top, and we roll down toward Boston College, where we part ways.

Back home I figure each successive 10 mile piece was faster than the prior one – maybe I'm not in such bad shape after all. On to the New Hampshire Marathon!

I've run one hundred miles in the past two weeks, including Mt. Pisgah, and now driving to Newfound Lake, I feel a little old. Heck, even my dog is getting old - nearly fifty in dog years. She'll be a geezer in six years when I turn 65. My hair's thinning, I've lost two molars, even this car I'm driving is getting on in miles.

By some magic when I park at the school in Bristol to register, the odometer stops exactly on seventy thousand miles – not a tenth more, not a tenth less. This has to be an omen of some kind. I wonder…

Soon we're on our way with scant New Hampshire fanfare, and I find myself in the back of the pack with a bunch of "Fifty Staters," aiming to run a marathon in all 50 states. The ones I've seen in past years are older, slower folks like me. I'm thinking a 4:45 would be respectable today, must conserve to avoid a late crash in the final miles.

I make the half on a 4:40 pace, right on schedule. After the turnaround, some guy heading out crosses by with an odd and surprising: "Hey you! I've got you in my sights, and I'm going to RUN YOU DOWN." This kind of challenge just doesn't happen in a country marathon, but I come right back with: "You're NEVER going to catch me."

Motivators – if you're open to them, they'll show. I begin to pick it up, now with a 200 yard lead, and not looking back, put the hammer down for about four miles, before I sneak a look to see if my challenger is anywhere in the zip code – he's out of sight.

I'm smoothin' it and feeling strong right now, remembering from the marathon website that the last eight miles are mostly downhill. Check the watch – "Hey, I could go sub 4:40 from here." For about an hour now there's been a guy in blue ahead of me, keeping a steady 300 yard lead. I think to close on this blue guy.

I pass people; none pass me. I'm running up all the short hills while others walk – closing slowly on the blue guy. At the end of the lake I know just two more miles to the finish. I'm 100 yards behind the blue guy, but at times he pulls ahead a few yards more distant. I think, "Maybe I can't catch him."

Then on the hill before the turn into the last mile, the blue guy slows to walk, slowing even more for the cop-guided traffic at the intersection. My chance: I charge up the hill, cutting the corner to cross. Then I'm shoulder to shoulder with him. He gives a little burst to show me he isn't cooked, but I know he is and I'm not.

The surge comes back – on call – same as on Heartbreak Hill, same as on Mt. Toby – just concentrate on relaxing, increase leg turnover, work complete full breaths, swing the arms, keep the head/neck erect – I sprint past the blue guy and others, all the way to a 4:32 finish.

Eight minute reverse splits! That dog, that car, they're not even half way done!

THREE

People often use the Bay State Marathon to make a qualifying time for Boston – Bay State's pretty flat and has the reputation of being fast. This one's going to be my last long training run before the Javelina Jundred 100 mile run on November 4th. With just two weeks between New Hampshire and Bay State, I taper some, running less than fifty miles, with complete rest the day before each event. This one today, I want a sub 4:30. For Boston, the 3:45 I'd need is well out of my reach.

The motivator comes to me in mile 11. I'd seen this young woman cruising ahead of me a few miles back. Feeling her pace slightly quicker, I'd dismissed the thought of marking her. Forty-five minutes later, she comes up from behind me – I must have gone by her at an aid station. Without forethought, I say, "Hey, I thought you were ahead of me." Not the slightest response from her, no recognition, even. I see the wires and know she's got music going, tunneled into her chosen zone. She draws away from me without noticeable effort, as I hold my existing pace.

There's a difference of about 20 seconds per mile, I figure. It would be nice to have that pace, but it's a little early to set the hook in myself. I believe I have the surge within, that it will emerge when called on, but I expected the call to come a little later, maybe mile 16 or so.

I pick up the pace. It's uncomfortable, but I hold it. Within minutes I'm settling into a higher tempo, closing on the music machine. There's a bridge, and I see the chance for separation, passing her before the turn. I've launched myself, even faster across the bridge.

Crossing the half at a 4:28 pace, I know there's risk I've played my hand too early. But I feel strong and continue to press it. Compared to New Hampshire, this is more aggressive; compared to Mt. Pisgah, I'm a different runner – clearly better conditioned.

In the six mile stretch before the next bridge crossing, I think, "Maintain this pace to the bridge at mile 19, then put the hammer down." There's a willowy guy ahead of me who resists getting buried, but I get him crossing the bridge. In these last seven miles, everyone around me is slowing while I'm pressing, advancing.

Mile 24 and the surge that I've played out carefully over the past 13 miles begins to fade. I'm left with myself and this empty body, driven only by will; stored energy is gone. The last bridge, then mile 26 and into the baseball stadium (Lowell Spinners), down the third base line, around the outfield track – good rock music cranking out – back down the right field foul line to the finish at home plate: a 4:20 finish – twelve minutes faster than New Hampshire and eight minute reverse splits again. Now that's something!

The perfect run happens when you maintain constant speed while gradually increasing effort to the maximum, near the finish. The perfect training cycle is one in which you push yourself hard enough to become stronger and faster without injury, to execute the targeted performance at the high end of expectations. Sisyphus this time around got the boulder very near the mountain top. Yes, I've lost a step or two, but I can still bring it.

———

JAVELINA JUNDRED – MCDOWELL MTN. PARK, AZ.
November 4-5, 2006

Soon after I introduce myself to Janet at Friday's race briefing, she asks, "Do you know your shirt's inside out?"

I do: "This is my 2006 Vermont 100 shirt. I DNF'd there and won't wear it right-side-out until I finish another 100 miler. Then I'll be redeemed, and my shirt, too."

That night, I rest more than sleep, going over the game plan, and over again. I've put myself into a high stakes test – must execute and must finish under the thirty hour time limit.

Two minutes before the 6 a.m. start on Saturday, I send my family telepathic greetings and feel their well wishes before closing the door on normal living. I'm wearing a clean shirt – Vermont lies stale and crumpled in my hotel room, waiting.

The first two miles of desert track lead to a gradual rise, strewn with loose rocks. I'm chatting with Tom, who time-marks the end of the plateau: "I like to clock these landmarks, because later on, the aid stations seem to get further apart." I mark accordingly.

The 15.3 mile loop has two aid stations at 5 mile intervals; closing the loop at the start/finish drop bag area, runners then reverse course (now counter-clockwise), again finding aid stations 5, then 10 miles out, before completing a full circuit.

One hundred seventeen runners carry high energy with big expectations. There's a lot of talk in the first couple hours. I'm purposely back of the pack, where unknowing first timers sprinkle bad karma on their chances by saying, "I hope I can finish."

The first aid station comes into view, maybe a mile distant. It's the same long look coming from the other direction, too – located on a ridge. I mark it at 1 hour 20 minutes, and the next at 1 and 20 also. The final third of the clockwise loop is a downhill coaster, which takes 15 minutes less time than the first two sections. Aid station volunteers have good runner awareness, so it's quick business to get in and out with a bite or two and something to drink.

Mile 14, Javelina Jundred

While the entire track is runnable, I conserve energy by walking most upgrades and the rocky section. Clear sky and temperatures in the 80's combine with ground radiation to make mid-day conditions mildly oppressive. I wear gaiters to keep sand and pebbles out, change socks when my feet start to feel gritty, and push electrolytes and fluid.

Six laps at four and a half hours each will put me at 27 hours with 9.2 miles to go – ample cushion to put 101 miles inside of 30 hours, if I hold to the plan. In prior 100's I've run the early miles more freely, walking in from mile 65 or 70 and still making the time limits. At Vermont this year, going out too fast is part of the reason I DNF'd at 50 miles, burning energy I couldn't find later in the day. This time I'm fixed into a more disciplined, slower pace I intend to keep throughout: six evenly paced legs, further broken down into 19 pieces of 5.1 miles (roughly), leaving a walk option for the last 4.2 miles.

Pam Reed offers valuable advice in her book *The Extra Mile* – when going long, make the distance seem less intimidating by reducing objectives into smaller sections: "I'm just focusing on reaching the next aid station" rather than "Jeez, I'm pretty gassed already and there's still 55 miles to go." Faster runners pass by me in both directions. Without pace discipline, I might get lured into outrunning my capabilities or become discouraged by their more advanced progress. When I get to the aid station at mile 35.7, people tell a faster pack, "You've already done 55 miles. It's a coast from here." Later in the race, I'm about 40 miles behind female winner Michelle Barton when she passes me. I can't count how many times Karl Meltzer goes by me on his way to a 15:25 winning finish, but I remind myself that his twice-as-fast pace is fine for him, but impossible for me.

Near the end of the third lap the sun is down, and the full moon's rising. I've been looking forward to this for the benefit of moderating temperatures and for the experience of running under moonlight. I carry lights, but find running without them affords better overall visibility most of the time. Some runners slavishly sweep their lights in front of them - automatons. One guy tells me "The moon isn't full" with scientific authority. For all their differences, these running people who fill the desert tonight are my brothers and my sisters.

Coming down into the rocky section about 11 p.m., I see dense sets of white blooming flowers on both sides of the trail – they were not here in my three prior passings. "Night blooming flowers emerging from cactus plants?" I wonder… Then again, on the return trip up the hill, lovely flowered corridors seem to light my way under the full moon – I'm awestruck, inspired, and energized by this spectacle. (Later I research: they are "Queen of the Night" or "Reina de la Noche" – magnificent !)

Once, I look up to admire the moon's beauty, just as a shooting star trails down to the east from the higher starry canopy. I think, even the automatons and the scientists must notice this beauty, must find this exhilarating, as I do.

Coyotes object to our being on their ground at night – different packs howl from dark distant places. I feel safe. Around 3 a.m., I'm holding a water bottle, now filled with hot soup to put warmth into my cold self, when I hear what first seems to be a rooster crowing – it's a vocally talented coyote shadowing me maybe 30 yards distant on the right. It sends clucks and yelps and gargled grrrs my way.

"Hey, you there – get offa my turf!" it seems to say. The coyote follows me for half a mile, verbally asserting its territorial claim. I feel not quite 100% safe, but continue to go along with my business. I'm nearing mile 75 and hard wired to finish.

I recall early morning training runs with my light – sometimes pointing it into the forest vegetation, I'd see a pair of animal eyes hiding there, watching me – a tangible reminder that for all we see, there's so much more that we don't, and we're often watched, more than we know.

Running 100's, reasons to drop out always come to me: sleepy, no energy, can't eat, blisters: worst of all – what's the point? This time I have rehearsed rebuttals to all my complaints, the most persuasive: "No matter how sorry you feel for yourself right now, you'll be much sorrier if you drop. It will haunt you for days and weeks and months to come. Push on, you sorry bastard."

The point is, to be for a short while outside the pull of humanity, without parents, or attachments, or normal life patterns; it's to be suspended in time and space, where for a while the physical self is subordinate to the mind's power, where distractions don't distract, where you feel part of a consciousness larger than simply living. Running 100's is a reach for immortality.

I see a tarantula. Instinct suddenly grounds me in a distinctly physical reaction: Fight? No, flight. I give her a wide berth, working the rock rubble just off the trail as she slowly goes about her hunt, no doubt warily keeping her many eyes on me – the smallish night predator startles a goliath. I regain composure, again locking into the trail, now with a little more lift in my step.

I'm in, then quickly out of the start/finish at 4:20 a.m. for the final 15.3 mile piece. Thirty hours will be close if I maintain the pace I've managed for the last 22 ½ hours. The first leg of the counter-clockwise lap is a gradual climb that I've walked twice before, and I walk it again: stay inside yourself, be patient – there's time. I make the aid station. No more pumpkin pie to savor; a bean burrito will do, and water in the CamelBak.

As the moon moves lower to the horizon, in the East a faint orange glow paints thin streaks between earth and sky. Before sunrise and moonset, the scene darkens, and I must use my light to see. I think, in this cosmic contest to illuminate, celestial battlers lurk in their respective corners, defaulting to darkness. Long after I've gone back to Boston, and all the others to their native dwellings, these desert animals and these stratospheric orbs will continue their rounds, mindless that we were ever there to witness them.

They say the dawn energizes an all-night runner: it's true. My pace quickens with the rising sun, but also from looking at my watch – there's little room for error. I'm on pace, but must hold it. I think, "How foolish it would be to go this long and this far, only to miss the cut-off by scant minutes." I run through the sloping rock-strewn path where I've only walked before, the blooming flowers gone, down toward the next aid station less than an hour distant. Must go. Must.

People coming up the slope in the final 9.2 mile loop offer encouragement, and I reciprocate. Javelina's set-up facilitates a spirit of team effort. Two runners tell me I'm a half-hour from the next aid station (mile 91.3) and that I can do it if I press on. Here comes Tom, then Catra and Xy: they make me a believer, more than I would be on my own.

I realize I haven't eaten for 3 hours – gotta feed the engine! At the start/finish turnaround I find orange slices and watermelon, good enough for the next three hours I figure, wheeling back out for the final 9.2 mile loop.

Once more, one last passage through the rock strewn climb – it seems now so cruelly sadistic. I know it's another test I can pass. I want this so badly. I reach the plateau that Tom and I marked 27 hours ago. I will never be in this place again. I will remember it indelibly. Now, can I see the aid station on the ridge? Must work, force a weak loping jog down, then up and down again through desert pathways – where, where is it?

I work, waiting for distance to pass under my feet; then I see it, not 10 minutes away. This time I'm directed to the right, down the Tonto trail, 4.2 miles to the finish. The aid station volunteer tells me I need to make 20 minute miles from here to clock under 30 hours. This I can do, mind tossing math around – even walking I can do it. Caution puts me into a shuffle, though - come too far, too long, to somehow miss it by a careless miscalculation. I think, "I'm here to run, and run I will, to ensure the completion I have wanted so much, these past hours, and days, and yes months: ever since 6:30 p.m. last July 15th, when I stepped out of the Vermont 100 trail and into the rescue truck."

In recent hours, shapes of desert objects have looked anomalous to me: brush collected along the trail as machinery, rocks of odd colors now squirrels scurrying, twisted cactus now motor vehicles. I approach a root structure, looking like a desiccated aviator – closer, I see that someone has put an old leather flying helmet on it to enhance the image. Locals here are richly humorous. I'm not so delusional after all, yet I can tell by the images that I conjure, my mind's eye stores a ready inventory of industrial shapes. Superficially at least, I'm an urban creature – too many years in the office, I guess.

Now comes the final stretch. I've passed this way 7 times, clocking it to be sure. I can walk in from here inside of 20 minutes, and I have 50. I run - this is now celebratory; finally – the strong finish with my goal close in hand. I know nothing more gratifying. Over the road and the final rise to see the finish line, I put down my strongest stride and bravest face to join myself with completion. I am whole again.

"I can't believe it's over" - my exact words, coming from unpremeditated origins, I think somewhere near my heart.

Thirty-eight years ago, I stripped off my Yale football uniform in a Harvard visitors' locker room, knowing I would never again take the form of a middle linebacker. It didn't happen overnight, but I adjusted nicely to the change.

Now, as I leave my 100 mile experiences behind me finally, I know this is the right decision. Time has outrun me, as I knew it would. I wanted to end it with a win – to end it on my own terms, and I have done that. For this I am thankful, with memories that I will cherish for as long as I live.

Javelina Jundred photo credits to Will LaFollette

CODA

I'm twenty-nine years old, working at a Mississippi River grain depot during harvest time. Trucks keep coming with corn for sale, and I'm writing purchase contracts for my employer hand over fist, the last one for eighty thousand bushels. Grain prices usually go down at harvest time, under the weight of new supplies being sold. I'm a grain trader; I sell corn with them. Mine is sold short in the futures market. Prices soon plummet. I quit my job, cover the short several weeks later, and use the profit as down payment for a house near Boston.

That's the house in the woods I trained out of, for the American Birkebeiner, my first ultra.

I'm thirty-five years old, working as a mutual fund portfolio manager in Boston. I switch the investments around to express a big bet that interest rates will go down. They do, and my mutual fund is a top performer that year.

I think I'm smart, but I'm just lucky. I think I can count on being lucky as well as being smart, but I can count on neither. It will take years before I know what I can count on.

It's 1998 and I'm reading Victor Niederhoffer's book *The Education of a Speculator*, published a year earlier. Victor shares secrets on how to trade money and win, how to beat even the Bank of Japan at its own game. I'm mesmerized by this. Victor tells about "hoodoos," the wannabes or has-beens who appear out from shadows to offer hot tips that never pan out, who hope to latch onto someone else's train of success, knowing they will never ride one of their own. "Avoid them," says Victor. In the same time frame, Victor Niederhoffer's hedge fund goes bust in an Asian currency crisis; his investors lose a fortune. "Who's the hoodoo now, Victor," I hum to myself. The question haunts me, as I follow my instinct into the culture of ultrarunning.

There, I learn that I was the hoodoo (Niederhoffer came back to run hedge fund money again – successfully) in so many ways that I did not know. In my personal and professional life, I acted the pretender, using false props and imaginary selves. Now, I leave all that behind, happily and with enough sense not to appear out from shadows to offer anyone hot tips.

Ultrarunning taught me how to lose my hoodoo, the one I recognized from reading Victor's book. Yet after many fulfilling runs, my pretender kept returning: on the bus to the Garden State 50 miler, as the fumbling distraction at Miwok in 2002, the "godfather" at Laurel Highlands, and the empty suit racking up incompletes during the spring and summer of 2006. But I never, never, ever gave up; I came back with focus to finish later that summer, and again in Arizona for that last Magical one hundred miler. Yes, I completed the victory lap I'd been dreaming of, after I saw that the clock would run me out of my hundred mile pilgrimages. Now I understand to let things simply happen, that I cannot make them or me into something that isn't, and that circumstances work out better when I remove selfish wishes from imagined outcomes.

Running on empty, ultrarunning's Magic, makes the puller, makes it easier to leave baggage behind, and easier to breathe freely. The practice of original thinking removes the mask that constantly tries to fit back on. Never, never, ever give up. Be mindful; there's always time, always time to get it right this time. Make time and dream big; it's all yours if you truly want it.

Form leads to emptiness and emptiness leads to form. For me it's not over, it's just beginning. From this point, there's no telling where it all might go.

LIST OF ULTRA STORIES

ECLECTIC BIBLIOGRAPHY

These are a few books I have read while training for ultramarathons. The categories describe ways the runner is encouraged to prepare, physically and mentally. Books from the categories "Adventure" and "War" generally find people in conditions far worse than in a typical ultra, thus lending perspective that no matter how bad one might feel while running, others have felt worse and survived. From "The Edge" and "The Center" there are many examples of thinking outside the box, which may help the runner prepare for unanticipated mental challenges that can come during the later stages of an ultra.

RUNNING

The Lore of Running – Dr Timothy Noakes

Racing the Antelope – Berndt Heinrich

Running Through the Wall – Neal Jamison

A Step Beyond: A Definitive Guide to Ultrarunning – Edited by Don Allison

Meditations from the Breakdown Lane – Jim Shapiro

Hardrock Fever – Robert Boeder

The Extra Mile – Pam Reed

Ultramarathon Man – Dean Karnazes

To the Edge – Kirk Johnson

Angeles Crest – Michael Modzelewski

Chi Running – Danny Dreyer

ADVENTURE

The Worst Journey in the World – Apsley Cherry Garrard

The Long Walk - Slavomir Rawicz

To The Top of the World – Reinhold Messner

A Voyage for Madmen – Peter Nichols

The Devil's Highway – Luis Alberto Urrea

Fielding's Hot Spots – Robert Young Pelton

The Hunter, The Hammer, And Heaven
– Robert Young Pelton

The Education of a Speculator – Victor Niederhoffer

WAR

Stalingrad – Anthony Beevor

Breakout – Martin Russ

Colder Than Hell – Joseph R Owen

We Were Soldiers Once and Young
– Harold Moore, Jos. Galloway

Master Chief – Gary Smith

Reflections of a Warrior- Franklin Miller

Dead Center – Ed Kugler

Inside Delta Force – Eric Haney

The Warrior Elite – Dick Couch

THE EDGE

Bone Games – Rob Schultheis

A Leg to Stand On – Oliver Sacks

The Beckoning Silence – Joe Simpson

Teaching a Stone to Talk – Annie Dillard

Racing the Sunset – Scott Simpson

Why God Won't Go Away – Andrew Newburg, M.D.

The Way Of The Peaceful Warrior – Dan Millman

The End Of Faith – Sam Harris

THE CENTER

The Universe In A Single Atom – Dalai Lama

The Heart Of The World – Ian Baker

The Way Of Zen – Alan Watts

Zen Mind, Beginner's Mind - Shunryu Suzuki

Not Always So – Shunryu Suzuki

Zen and the Brain – James Austin

The Neuroscience of Human Relationships
– Louis Cozolino